THE OXFORD AND CAMBRIDGE CLUBS IN LONDON

The Oxford and Cambridge Clubs in London

John Thole

LONDON

1992

To John Posford, who first interested me in the Club's affairs

First published in 1992
by The United Oxford and Cambridge University Club
in association with
Alfred Waller Limited
Publishers
Henley-on-Thames Oxon

British Library Cataloguing in Publication Data
A catalogue record for this book is available
from the British Library

ISBN 1-872474-01-2

Produced for the publishers by
John Taylor Book Ventures
Hatfield Herts

Made and printed in Great Britain.
by The Bath Press

Frontispiece:
Vestibule of O&C, c.1960

Contents

Acknowledgments

I wish to record my gratitude to Messrs James Bishop, Robert Holland, David Morgan, John Posford and Eric Vallis for private information. I have also received valuable information from Mr Andrew Dobson about the Harington Judgment. The Librarian, Mrs Chandler, has been unfailingly helpful in guiding me through the club archives.

Particular thanks are due to Mr Richard Chown for editing the illustrations.

John Thole

The author and publishers would like to thank the following for permission to quote or to reproduce photographs:
The Bodley Head for the quotation from Lord Wolfenden's *Turning Points*
Dr Malcolm Graeme for the quotation from 'Suffolk Street in the 1940s'
Greater London Record Office and History Library (illustration on p. 5)
Greater London Photograph Library (frontispiece and illustrations on pp. 60 and 90)
National Portrait Gallery (illustration on p. 14)
Mr & Mrs John Ryan and Philip Wilson Publishers Ltd (illustration on p. 59)
Winds magazine and Hirotsugu Okamura (colour plate 6)

Foreword

Some three years ago the author diffidently approached my predecessor and suggested that, with time on his hands, he would if encouraged be prepared to research and write a history of the Club and its place in London clubland. The General Committee welcomed the idea, readily offered support and full access to club records, and expressed its intention to seek publication of the completed work.

John Bernard Thole was born on 22 August 1930. He was educated at Oundle and Trinity Hall, where he graduated in 1953, taking his MA in 1957. He served with the Green Jackets, then taught history as a civilian instructor at the Royal Naval College, Greenwich. In 1966 he became a lecturer at Imperial College, University of London, where he remained until 1988, although continuing with some teaching for another two years.

On retirement he devoted much of his time to researching and writing this book in the Club he so loved and which he joined in 1966. He gave unselfishly of his time and served for a number of years on the library sub-committee and was latterly a member of the General Committee.

Reserved and dignified by nature, he was a generous man with an acute intelligence and a dry, laconic wit. He died on Christmas morning 1991 after a short illness stoically borne just two months after completing, with a sense of personal fulfilment, the text of this book.

Stephen Matthews
Chairman

United Oxford and Cambridge University Club
March 1992

Illustrations

COLOUR PLATES (appearing between pages 102 and 103)

BLACK AND WHITE ILLUSTRATIONS

Abbreviations used in the text and notes

UUC   The United University Club, Suffolk Street
OC   The Oxford and Cambridge University Club, Pall Mall
NUC   The New University Club, St James's Street

GCM   General Committee Minutes
AGM(M)   Annual General Meeting (Minutes)
EGM(M)   Extraordinary General Meeting (Minutes)
SGM(M)   Special General Meeting (Minutes)

Chapter I

Foundations

The nineteenth century saw an extraordinary proliferation of London clubs. At its beginning there were scarcely half-a-dozen with perhaps 1,200 members between them: by its end, it has been estimated, there were probably at least two hundred, with a total of over 200,000 members.

Nowhere is this burgeoning better illustrated than by the multiplicity of clubs catering solely for the members of Oxford and Cambridge. The first to be founded was the United University Club in 1821. Nine years later there was need for another, so the Oxford and Cambridge University Club was founded in 1830. The length of their waiting lists eventually led to the establishment in St James's Street of a third in 1864, known as the New University Club, and this lasted until 1938 when it amalgamated at Suffolk Street with the UUC.

And although their records have unfortunately perished, references in the archives of the first three confirm that there were a fourth and a fifth. One was called the Junior Oxford and Cambridge Club, which from 1879 until 1892 shared No. 8 St James's Square with three other clubs – the Vine, the York and the Junior Travellers'. The fifth was the New Oxford and Cambridge Club, probably founded in 1885 or a little before. We know this because in March of that year they wrote to the Oxford and Cambridge Club asking if it would take in their members until their own club house would be ready in May, 1886 – a request which was refused for lack of space. This new club house was in Pall Mall, 'within two houses' of the Oxford and Cambridge

Club, a circumstance which, given the similarity of their names, led to a good deal of confusion over the correct delivery of the mail. The New Oxford and Cambridge lasted until 1933, when it sought amalgamation with the New University Club in St James's Street. That never happened because of the disparity in subscriptions and because by then, as the committee of the NUC gently put it, 'the terms of their membership were very broad', meaning presumably that by then it was by no means confined to members of Oxford and Cambridge.

In addition there was the City University Club, a luncheon club founded in the late nineteenth century and which survives to this day, but is no longer exclusively Oxbridge.

The United University Club

Thatched House, St James's-street
June 30, 1821

Resolved
That a Club be established under the name of the UNITED UNIVERSITY CLUB.

That the Club consist of 1000 Members, 500 of the University of Oxford, 500 of the University of Cambridge, who have regularly proceeded to a Degree, after at least one year's Residence; or who have been admitted to any College or Hall in either University shall have been resident members during two years at least.

That no member shall be admitted while a Resident Undergraduate.

That each Member shall pay on admission Ten guineas, to be appropriated to the establishment of a suitable House.

That the Annual Subscription be Five Guineas.

Thus, pithily, did the first of the university clubs in London come into being. The Resolutions bear five signatures: first, Joseph Phillimore of Christ Church, who combined his membership of Parliament with being Regius Professor of Civil

Law at Oxford. Then came the names of Edward Bastard, MP, of Christ Church, the Hon. W. Cust, MP, the Hon. George Lamb, MP (both of Trinity, Cambridge) and the Reverend W. F. Baylay (St John's, Cambridge), Chaplain to the House of Commons. It seems reasonable to assume that it was these who had taken the lead in bringing the meeting about.

The Thatched House where they met was not a club but a tavern – the club of that name was not founded until 1865 – but it had a room or rooms where various societies could meet, such as the Society of Dilettanti, the Literary Club and the Yacht Club, which later became the Royal Yacht Squadron.[1] The tavern survived till 1843.

The original trustees and committee, thirty in number, bore a strongly political flavour: no less than sixteen were Members of one House of Parliament or the other and included two past or future Chancellors of the Exchequer (the Marquess of Lansdowne and T. Spring Rice), a future Prime Minister (the Earl of Aberdeen) and the current speaker of the House of Commons, Charles Manners-Sutton. The senior trustee was the Duke of Northumberland, who was to become Chancellor of Cambridge in 1840, and was according to Greville 'an eternal talker and a prodigious bore'. A certain academic *ton* was provided by the presence on the committee of Mr Serjeant Frere, Master of Downing and Vice-Chancellor of Cambridge in 1819, the aforementioned Regius Professor of Civil Law at Oxford, Joseph Phillimore, and for good measure the Head Masters of Westminster and Charterhouse. As well as these two at least three others of the committee were in holy orders.

They must have applied themselves prodigiously for by the time of the Annual General Meeting in 1823 the membership was full and already there was a waiting list of nearly 300, and temporary premises had been acquired at No. 106 Pall Mall. A start had already been made on the building of a permanent club house at the corner of Suffolk Street and Pall Mall East.

Pall Mall had for over half a century been the centre of fashionable club and coffee house life. Brooks's and Boodle's (preceded by Almack's till 1764) had started life there, though Boodle's moved to St James's Street in 1783 and Brooks's had already done so in 1778: in 1822 the building was occupied by the recently-formed Travellers' Club. Others, such as Goostree's, the Cocoa Tree and the Macaroni Club had briefly flourished there. The Smyrna Coffee House, mentioned by Swift in *The Tatler* and *The Spectator*, had been just to the east of Crown Passage. By the early nineteenth century Pall Mall was, according to Charles Ollier, a 'stately aristocratic-looking street' with 'private mansions fit for the residence of the wealthy and the noble'. The east end of it, however, was not so smart as the St James's Palace end, being 'bordered with filthy alleys, inhabited by abandoned characters'.[2] Suffolk Street lies in the angle between the Haymarket – still until 1830 London's principal market for hay and straw – and Pall Mall East, just where it debouches into what is now Trafalgar Square, but which was at the time the club was founded a maze of slums around St Martin-in-the-Fields, known as Porridge Island. On the site of the National Gallery were the royal stables, moved there by Henry VIII in 1534 – handily close to the Haymarket.

To find an architect the committee had not far to look, for among the founder members of the club was William Wilkins, who had been at Caius and was sixth wrangler in 1800. He was already established as an architect in university circles for his work at Downing between 1806 and 1811, and in 1822 was just completing work on the bridge, hall, Provost's Lodge and stone screen at King's. He is usually associated with the architecture of the Greek Revival, though his buildings at King's show that when necessary he could turn his hand with all the fluency of his Victorian successors to the Gothic or whatever else was called for.[*] However, in cooperation with his associate, J. P. Gandy-Deering, Wilkins provided for the committee a logical and

[*] Other buildings by Wilkins include Haileybury College (1806), Grange Park, Hampshire (1809), University College London (1827–8), St George's Hospital (1827–8) and the National Gallery (1832–8), where his style may have been somewhat cramped by the obligation to make use of the heavy porch from Carlton House, by then demolished. The last, with its insignificant pepper-pot dome, is perhaps his least successful work, though at least he had the vision to set back the portico so as to retain the vista towards St Martin-in-the-Fields from Pall Mall.

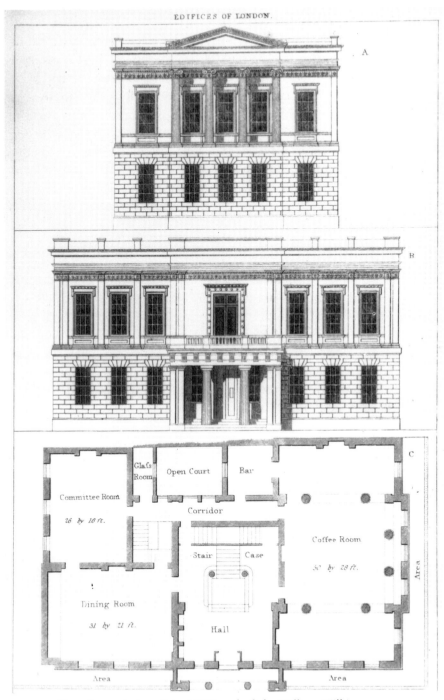

EDIFICES OF LONDON.

A

B

Glass Room

Open Court

Bar

Committee Room

26 by 16 ft.

Corridor

Stair   Case

Coffee Room

50 by 28 ft.

Area

Dining Room

31 by 21 ft.

Hall

Area   Area

C

Elevation and plan of the UUC, as built by William Wilkins

handsome adaptation of a villa plan for the new club house. The style was Doric and Ionic and the accommodation provided two coffee rooms, drawing rooms, a smoking room, libraries and a card room and a map room. There were dressing rooms but no bedrooms, a committee room and the usual provision for butler's pantry, servants' hall, steward's and housekeeper's rooms, kitchen, still room, glass room and hall porter's closet.

The committee seem to have been well pleased with the result, and recorded their satisfaction in their Annual Report for 1823.

> The Committee in presenting the Annual Report on the Affairs of the Club, conceive that they cannot discharge that duty in a more acceptable manner to the General Meeting than by reverting to that well grounded expectation expressed last year on the progress of the Building which has been so completely realized, both in respect to the time stipulated and the perfect execution of the work.
>
> ... It is on these grounds that the Committee think themselves called upon to recommend to the General Meeting to confer on Mr Wilkins and on Mr Gandy a deserved mark of their approbation by proposing a vote of thanks in such terms as will make it most valuable to Mr Wilkins (himself a Member of the Club) and in the case of Mr Gandy by admitting him by their vote as an Honorary Member, a tribute to his taste and acquirements, and to his unceasing attention to the interior decoration of the Building and to the assistance he has voluntarily given in designs for the Furniture and Ornaments of the House.[3]

The proposal was agreed unanimously, as well it might be: the club house had been completed not only on time but within £300 of the original estimate of £14,050.

As even the most perfunctory glance at the original list of members for 1822, which has happily survived, will reveal, they were a distinguished crowd. First there were the grandees: Lord Grenville, the Chancellor of Oxford, the Duke of Gloucester, Chancellor of Cambridge, the Dukes of Grafton, Northumberland and Rutland, and the Earl of Aberdeen. How far any of these took an active interest in the club, or whether they simply lent their names in a spirit of aristocratic patronage, is hard to say. In all, some fifty-one peers and about the same number of baronets or knights appear on the list.

Classified by calling or occupation the most numerous category by far were the clergy. Starting with the Archbishop of Canterbury and four bishops, 284 of the thousand original members were in holy orders. Not all, of course, were necessarily beneficed, for many academics were ordained. Though fictional in form, Anthony Trollope's description of the scene when affairs of great ecclesiastical moment were to be debated cannot be far from the truth. *

Next most numerous were the politicians. Though by no means a political club, Members of Parliament seem to have made themselves at home there, possibly because they had nowhere else to go, for the older political clubs – Brooks's and White's – had now lost much of their political connotation since the deaths of Pitt and Fox, and because the new ones – the Reform and the Carlton – had not yet been founded. In the 1820s and 1830s it might theoretically have been possible to find a substantial portion of the cabinet dining there. Robert Peel, the Member for Oxford University was, at the time the club was formed, the Home Secretary: Palmerston, the Member for Cambridge University, was Secretary at War in successive administrations. It is hard to imagine Peel being particularly clubbable, for he was reserved and shy and threw out no genial glow to those around him, but Palmerston, on the other hand, was a friendly presence and used the club quite a bit. Peel became a trustee in 1825 and remained one till his death in 1850: Palmerston was elected to the committee in 1824. Canning, Vansittart (created Lord Bexley in 1823), C. W. W. Wynn and the Marquess Camden, all founder members, served in Lord Liverpool's ministry: when Canning became Prime Minister for five months in 1827, Sturgess Bourne, the Marquess of Lansdowne and Palmerston served in his cabinet.

---

* 'Upon the present occasion London was full of clergymen. The specially clerical clubs – the Oxford and Cambridge, the Old University, and the Athenaeum – were black with them.' *Phineas Redux*, vol. 1, ch. xxxiii (World's Classics ed., vol. 2, p. 290). Though he lived for a while in Suffolk Street and was a keen member of the Athenaeum and the Garrick, Trollope was never a member of the United University, for which he was not eligible. There are several references to it in the novels, always as the 'Old' University. However, his father, T. A. Trollope, was a founder member.

Though an inveterate founder of clubs, the Duke of Wellington was not an original member at Suffolk Street, since he was not eligible until he became Chancellor of Oxford in 1835, whereupon he was made a member without ballot at his own request. But five out of the thirteen members of his cabinet, formed in January 1828, were. As was only to be expected, the founding of more specifically political clubs led to a weakening in the link between the United University Club and Westminster: nevertheless, as many as ten prime ministers were to be members.*

It was natural enough, although the club and the universities were and always remained completely independent of each other, that a good many dons became members. Fourteen heads of houses – seven from each university – are to be found on the original list, including the Warden of All Souls (who doubled as Bishop of Oxford) and the Master of Christ's, Cambridge (who doubled as Bishop of Bristol), the Provost of King's (George Thackeray, a cousin of the novelist), Edward Copleston, the Provost of Oriel, and Thomas le Blanc, the Master of Trinity Hall, 'a devotee of port and a martyr to gout', according to Charles Crawley.*†

Other fellows are less readily identifiable, though they certainly included Thomas Calvert, Norrisian Professor at Oxford, Charles Lloyd, Regius Professor of Divinity, Henry Milman, Professor of Poetry and Sir Christopher Pegge, Regius Professor of Medicine. Further links existed through the Members of Parliament who sat for the two universities, the first being Peel and Richard Heber, for Oxford, and Palmerston and John Smyth, for Cambridge.

The fourth element in this great new wedge of middle- and

* Namely, Canning, Wellington, Grey, Peel, Melbourne, Aberdeen, Palmerston, Gladstone and Baldwin. Campbell-Bannerman and Attlee were members of the Oxford and Cambridge. Palmerston and Gladstone joined both. Wellington and Macmillan were elected to both in their capacity as Chancellors of Oxford.
† Copleston later became Bishop of Llandaff. It was claimed that he was the last person in England to be robbed by a highwayman (in 1799, between Beaconsfield and Uxbridge). Le Blanc was Master twice, 1815–18 and 1818–43. He had resigned in 1818 rather than face being Vice-Chancellor, but agreed a few days later to be re-elected, and in fact was Vice-Chancellor, 1824–5.

upper-class professionals who would dominate the nation's life in the nineteenth century were the lawyers. Heading the list (almost literally, for his is the second name on it) was Sir Charles Abbott, Chief Justice of the Court of King's Bench, and the roll of members bristles with the names of Serjeants at Law, Masters in Chancery, King's Counsel.

Finally, there is discernible one perhaps unexpected but nonetheless colourful category of members, the headmasters of nearly all the leading public schools of the day. *Primus inter pares*, perhaps, was the Reverend John Keate, Headmaster of Eton from 1809 to 1834 – 'Flogger' Keate, who once birched a hundred boys in the lower fifth, and on another occasion all the confirmation candidates by mistake. He tried to flog Eton into submission but apparently failed, for the noise from his classes was said to be deafening.[5]* There was the Reverend John Sleath, High Master of St Paul's,[6]† the Reverend Edmund Goodenough, Head Master of Westminster, the Reverend John Russell, Headmaster of Charterhouse, J. T. Allen, Warden of Dulwich, the Reverend Joseph Hallett, Principal of the East India College, and the Reverend George Butler, Headmaster of Harrow, against whom, in 1805, Byron had led an uprising in which the boys burnt his desk and actually laid a trail of gunpowder down a passage before thinking better of blowing up the whole school. To these at least, the new club in Suffolk Street must have seemed a haven of tranquillity.

With such members, how could the club possibly fail? With membership lists full and an ever-lengthening waiting list, the committee felt sufficiently confident in their report to the 1824 Annual General Meeting to increase the entrance fee in future for

---

* 'He was a fantastic figure: five-foot tall, strong as a bull and equipped, under a high cocked hat like Napoleon, with enormous shaggy red eyebrows, great angry tufts, so long that he used them like arms or hands when he wished to point at something. His temper was terrifying: he would get "so inflamed in the face, and foamed and spurted from the mouth" so ferociously that it was like someone in a fit.' However, he was not unpopular with the boys.

† He once told a parent 'At St Paul's we teach nothing but the classics, nothing but Latin and Greek. If you want your son to learn anything else you must have him taught at home, and for this purpose we give three half-holidays a week.' So much for the national curriculum.

all new members from ten to twenty guineas, and again in 1826 to twenty-five guineas – an enormous sum in today's money.

So the club seems fairly quickly to have assumed the even tenor of its way for the next hundred-and-fifty years, not much disturbed by the passing scene; tranquil, not particularly sociable, rather donnish – the sort of place where members were more likely to dine alone over a newspaper rather than in company; where the food was adequate to the undemanding tastes of the members, but with a renowned cellar. Later, when Gladstone joined, it became his favourite club 'where he might be seen resting at times over a plain chop with a Homer or book of divinity set up before him to read when he dined.'[7] He would never, apparently, yield to suggestions to join the Athenaeum because he preferred the UUC.[8]

The Oxford and Cambridge University Club

By 1828 the UUC had allowed its membership to rise from the original thousand to 1,130 and the club house was bulging at the seams. Already there was a proposal to build a new one, though it came to nothing. Since the waiting lists for both Oxford and Cambridge candidates were growing longer and longer, it was entirely logical that those upon them decided that, rather than go on waiting, they would form a new university club, and this they did: 'At a numerous Meeting of Members of the Universities of Oxford and Cambridge, held at the British Coffee House Cockspur Street, on Monday 17th May 1830 – Viscount Palmerston in the Chair – It was resolved That a Club be formed consisting of Members of the Universities of Oxford and Cambridge to be called "The Oxford and Cambridge University Club".'[9]

It was to have six hundred members, three hundred from each university. Members must have taken a degree or passed the examinations for a degree, must have resided for at least two years and must have permanently discontinued their residence. Every original member was to pay ten guineas entrance money and an annual subscription of five guineas: for later members the entrance fee was to be fifteen guineas.

Lord Palmerston
The portrait after Cruikshank, in the coffee room

The committee was to consist of three trustees and twenty-six other members (three to be resident in each university), with a quorum of five. It would be for them to take a house for not more than eleven years. All princes of the blood royal, privy councillors, bishops and judges being otherwise duly qualified were to be admitted as original or supernumerary members. Election of members was to be by the committee, three black balls to exclude.*

Between 19 May and 16 June the committee met no fewer than nine times: on 17 June another General Meeting was held, again with Palmerston in the chair, to apprise the members of what the committee had so far done, which was not a little. Trustees had been appointed; candidates had been balloted for,† rules and regulations had been completed; an advertisement for a house had been placed in *The Times* and *The Morning Post*. This had elicited several offers, including the Clarendon Hotel and Sir John Beckett's house at No. 15 St James's Square.‡ It had been inspected and in the committee's view 'the House in St James's Square is in almost every way suitable for the purpose of the Club'.[10] Negotiations had been entered into and they had agreed to take the house, partly furnished, at £1,200 for eighteen months, rates and taxes included.

At this meeting they decided to extend somewhat the roll of supernumerary members to include the Speakers of Lords and Commons and the Chancellors, High Stewards and MPs of both universities, being duly qualified: this included any who had held

---

* On certain of these points the committee had second thoughts when they came to draft the rules and regulations a month later. Membership, they proposed, should be open not just to those who had proceeded to a degree but to those who had resided for two years (this was partly to take account of the fact that many who went up never bothered to take a degree and partly because at that time noblemen got a degree automatically after two years without examination). Further, they decided that in future election to the Club should be ballot of the members as a whole: ballots would be held every Thursday from February to July when the House was sitting, between three and four o'clock. At least twenty votes were required for each candidate and one black ball in every ten was to exclude.

† By the date of this meeting, candidates already exceeded 600, 467 had already been elected.

‡ Re-numbered No. 18. The house stood at the north corner of King Street and St James's Square.

those posts in the past. A further category of honorary membership was to include graduates of Trinity College, Dublin who
were archbishops, bishops, judges of the superior courts in
Ireland, the Attorney or Solicitor General for Ireland, and any
KC or barrister who was an MP – provided that they paid an
annual subscription.

They further decided that the club house was to be open from 8
a.m. to 2 a.m. (though those members already in the house by 2
a.m. need not leave). Lest this lead to loose living and bring the
club into disrepute, they resolved 'that no games of Loo or Haz-
ard shall on any account be played, nor Dice used in the Club
House; and that no game shall be allowed to be played on Sundays.' Moreover, no bets were to exceed one guinea.[11]

On 21 June the committee met for the first time in their new
club house (for the first few weeks they had rented a room at the
British Coffee House) and set about the task of interviewing and
appointing those key members of a club's staff, the secretary, the
butler and the hall porter. On 5 July 1830 the club opened its
doors to members for the first time.

Since it was first built in the 1670s St James's Square had been a
fashionable address. When Whitehall Palace was destroyed by
fire in 1698 the Court had moved to St James's Palace: by 1700
the Square contained six dukes and seven earls. It was at No. 16
(now the East India Club) that the Prince Regent had received the
news of Wellington's victory at Waterloo. After 1815, though,
the great families began to move either to Mayfair or Belgravia
and the clubs moved in.[12]

Whether it was because the committee were now exhausted, or
simply because the members were perfectly happy there, no further effort to find a permanent home for the club was made for
some years. Instead the committee took a five year lease on Sir
John Beckett's house, offering £900 *per annum*: Beckett de-
murred, so the committee offered £1,000, which was accepted.
Certain domestic matters required attention: the drains and cess
pools of the house needed to be repaired and cleaned: in April
1831, during the Reform riots, the Mob had smashed the windows. The committee decreed 'that the proper notice be affixed to

Sir Robert Smirke
Engraved by W. Daniell from the portrait by George Dance

the Church Door to claim compensation for breakage', but by June had decided 'that no further Expense be incurred in prosecuting the claim'.[13] Doubtless to help meet such expenses it was decided in December to admit fifty more members (they had already been empowered to do this by a Special General Meeting in March). In April 1832 the committee agreed to increase the subscription by one guinea (to six) 'if the Annual General Meeting approved' (it did).[14]

By now the club employed twenty-two servants together with the Steward and the Secretary, and it was decided to take over the running of the kitchen department, which appears hitherto to have been contracted to an outside caterer.

What seems to have prompted the committee to further action towards establishing a permanent home for itself was an offer in March 1934 by Sir John Beckett to sell them his house. This offer was declined and the following month they resolved 'that application be made to the Commissioners of Woods and Forests for the refusal of certain ground on the South Side of Pall Mall from Nos 71 to 76 inclusive'.[15] They decided to recommend to the Annual General Meeting to give notice to quit St James's Square and to take the Pall Mall site, at the same meeting resolving 'that a Union of this Club with the United University Club is desireable'.[16] However, the latter proposal was dropped when Sir Robert Smirke, the architect they had chosen to appoint, gave it as his opinion that the Pall Mall site was too small to build a club house large enough to accommodate the combined membership, but that it would be suitable for a house for up to 1,200 members. He was duly instructed to prepare plans and estimates, and at the 1835 Annual General Meeting the committee was authorised to take the site and spend up to £27,000.

Robert Smirke was by this date a well-established architect with an immense practice. The son of the painter of the same name, he had studied briefly in Sir John Soane's office before travelling in Germany, Italy and Greece, from which last he was to derive his main inspiration. He had been responsible for the Doric re-building of Covent Garden Opera House (1808–09), several country houses (including Lowther Castle in Westmoreland and Eastnor Castle in Herefordshire), the Royal College of Physicians and the Union Club in Trafalgar Square and the General Post Office in St Martin-le-Grand. The last two are now demolished; what he is best remembered for today is the British Museum (begun in 1823 and completed in 1847). It could almost have been by Wilkins, for, like him, Smirke was a devotee of the Greek Revival.

It is sometimes asserted that Robert Smirke's brother, Sydney,* had a hand in the design of the Oxford and Cambridge Club. It is not impossible, for the club made both honorary members and at a later date he was the club's consultant architect; but the evidence is circumstantial. The club records give no sign that more than one architect was involved, and certainly all the dealings were with Sir Robert.

The site of 71–76 Pall Mall was at this stage occupied by a house (previously three houses) which had been acquired in 1725 by Sir Robert Walpole, principally with the object of frustrating the intentions of the Duchess of Marlborough, who wanted to obtain direct access to Marlborough House from Pall Mall, since she had recently been denied the privilege she had previously enjoyed of travelling there in her coach through St James's Park.† By 1740 the house was in the hands of (Sir) Edward Walpole, Sir Robert's second son. In about 1778 he was succeeded by his natural daughter, Laura, and the house subsequently passed to her son, Frederick Keppel, who died in 1830.

Smirke wasted little time: his plans were placed before the committee and accepted with only minor changes, though they were at first doubtful about the front elevation and asked whether it might be changed to a different style. Smirke appears to have

* Sydney Smirke (1798–1877) designed the Carlton Club in Pall Mall (destroyed during the Second World War), the Conservative Club in St James's Street and the circular Reading Room in the British Museum.
† 'The Late Duchess of Marlborough ... intended to have opened a way to it from Pallmall, directly in front, as is evident from the manner in which the court yard is finished; but Sir Robert Walpole having purchased the house before it, and being upon no good terms with the Duchess, she was prevented in her design.' *London and Its Environs Described*, printed by R. and J. Dodsley in Pall Mall, 1761; quoted in F. H. W. Sheppard. *Survey of London*, vol. XXIX, pt 1, p. 379. Hence today's rather poky entrance to Marlborough House, between Marlborough Road and Hambro's Bank.

convinced them that this would not be possible without entirely redesigning the interior, for his proposals were formally accepted on 30 July 1835. Six tenders from contractors were received, the successful one being made by Messrs Grissell and Peto of York Road Lambeth, in the sum of £24,130 (getting on for twice the cost of the United University Club). The old buildings on the site were demolished and the ground handed over to Smirke on 5 November 1835.

If the extra bedroom storey, the area railings and the flambeaux are disregarded, Smirke's original design for the Pall Mall elevation has remained unchanged (the flambeaux, referred to simply as six 'columns', were added in 1872 and the bedroom storey in 1912). The bas-reliefs in the panels over the windows were designed by Robert Smirke, RA, the architect's father, and carried out by William Nicholl. Also virtually unaltered are the main public rooms on the first and second floors (that is, the morning room, now the members' bar, the coffee room, the smoking room and the North and South Libraries). The wine bar was formerly the strangers' dining room. The basement, mezzanine and the upper floors have, however, been considerably altered and chopped about to meet the changing needs of the members, as has the main staircase, which was elaborately altered by Sir Reginald Blomfield in 1907.*

The site, in common with the others on the south side of Pall Mall,† is held on a Crown lease from the Commissioners for Woods and Forests (now known as the Crown Commissioners), which probably accounts for the fact that all the architectural distinction of the street lies on this side, whereas the north side, being in private hands with narrow frontages, is an architectural gallimaufry of little merit.

---

* It is assumed here that most readers will be familiar with the building as it is today. However, for any who want a fuller and more technical architectural description, one will be found in the admirably scholarly *Survey of London*, vol. XXIX, pt. 1.
† All, that is, except for No. 79, where Nell Gwynne lived and which has been in private hands since 1676 because when Charles II offered her a long lease, she insisted on a freehold because she 'had always conveyed free under the Crown and always would'.

View of the O&C, c. 1840

Eighteenth-century and Regency club houses, which just about included the UUC, tended to be modest in scale, emulating a gentleman's private London residence. In keeping with the tendency among the later clubs, Smirke's Oxford and Cambridge Club was conceived on a much more palatial scale: by no stretch of the imagination could the coffee room, say, or the smoking room be rooms in a private house.

According to *The British Almanac of The Society for the Diffusion of Useful Knowledge for the Year 1838*, 'the foundations were commenced in November 1835, and the whole building is engaged to be completed by Christmas of the present year [1837].' In fact it took just a little longer, but the building was completed in only twenty-six months. The committee had hoped it would be ready by November 1837 so that the members would be able to view from their new vantage point the new Queen's state drive to the City to dine with the Lord Mayor, but Smirke advised against it, on the grounds that 'the work in its present state would be subject to injury from any great influx of Members'.[17] However, they had not long to wait: on 18 January 1838 the committee was able to hold its first meeting in the new club house, and on Monday, 5 February it was opened for the reception of members.

Who were they, and how, if at all, did they differ in character and composition from the members at the other club? Unfortunately in this case the original list of members has not survived, but from the earliest which does – that for 1839 – it seems clear that, as at Suffolk Street, the clergy were the largest single category: 190 out of what had by then become a total of a thousand members. Members of Parliament are again well represented, though not so plentifully as at Suffolk Street: forty-two ordinary and six of the honorary members were MPs, to whom may be added at least some of the dozen peers. The Law and the Universities are again well represented.

The original trustees were the Marquess of Chandos, who later became Duke of Buckingham;* Lord Cavendish, subsequently

---

* Known as 'the Farmers' Friend' for repealing the Malt Tax.

The Duke of Devonshire
The portrait by G. Sebel, in the morning room

seventh Duke of Devonshire and Chancellor of Cambridge,* and Sir Robert Inglis,† who had become a Member of Parliament for Oxford University in 1829 when he defeated Peel.

The original committee numbered among its members the Lord Chancellor, the Earl of Ossory, Lord Palmerston and six in holy orders. Among the original membership generally, certain names stand out. There was for example the Reverend B. H. Kennedy, Headmaster of Shrewsbury, later Regius Professor of Greek at Cambridge, and the author of *The Public School Latin Primer*, familiar to many later generations of schoolboys. There was Richard Chenevix-Trench, later Archbishop of Dublin, who is said to be the person who first suggested the compilation of the *Oxford English Dictionary*, and the third Earl of Egremont, friend of Palmerston and patron of Turner and Constable, who assembled the fine collection at Petworth, and was rich and generous enough to spend for sixty years £20,000 a year on charity. Some were courtiers, like Sir Frederick Trench, ADC to George IV and William IV and MP for Cambridge, who originally planned the Thames Embankment; and the fourth Baron Talbot of Malahide, who was Lord in Waiting to Queen Victoria. There was Edward Boscawen, created Earl of Falmouth at George IV's coronation, who had been Lord Winchelsea's second in his duel with the Duke of Wellington in 1829. The last surviving original member was to be John Temple Leader, a member for seventy-five years and eventually Father of the Club, who survived until 1903. He lived in Florence, where he occupied his time with restoring the gigantic castle of Vincigliata. Though it is sometimes alleged that he was, the Duke of Wellington was not a founder member: he was elected in 1838 in his

---

* According to the present Duchess, '. . . a scholar, a serious, quiet man, who disliked social life as much as his predecessor enjoyed it. He was a widower for fifty-one years and never ceased to grieve for his dead wife. It is said he never smiled again after she died. One has the feeling he did not smile much before.' *The House*, p. 31. His portrait in the club house rather confirms her impression, and somehow one is not surprised to learn that he spent his honeymoon teaching his wife geometry.
† A stern opponent of the admission to Oxford of Papists and Dissenters, '. . . the strength of whose sentiments, the force and occasional ferocity of whose epithets were the more noticeble from the bland meakness of his manner and the melting softness of his voice.' T. H. S. Escott. *Club Makers and Club Members*, p. 239.

The Duke of Wellington
The portrait by J. Lucas, in the morning room

capacity as Chancellor of Oxford. *

To this list of notables among the founder members must be added one notoriety. This was William Smith O'Brien, the Member of Parliament for Limerick. In 1848 – a nervous year for the ruling classes everywhere – the Government had brought in a bill for the better security of the Crown and Government, making all written incitement to insurrection or resistance to law a felony punishable by transportation. Smith O'Brien was by now the recognised leader of the Young Ireland Party, seeking Irish Home Rule. He was in Ireland leading the agitation and came into collision with the Police. *Habeas Corpus* was suspended in Ireland and a warrant issued for O'Brien's arrest. In the brush with the Police in which a few of his followers were killed or wounded, O'Brien was arrested. When the committee met on 2 August a 'letter addressed by F. Goulburn Esq to the Committee was received and read. Mr Goulburn suggests that Mr Smith O'Brien, in open mutiny against Her Majesty, ought to be expelled from the Club'. The committee, however, did not agree and resolved 'that it is not expedient that the Committee should comply with Mr Goulburn's suggestion'.[18]

At his trial on 9 October before a special commission at Clonmel in Tipperary O'Brien was found guilty of treason and, as the law then required, was sentenced to be hung, beheaded and quartered, though in the event this was commuted to transportation for life to Australia. This was too much for certain members, thirty-two of whom sent a certificate to the committee demanding a special general meeting, saying that 'the conduct of Mr William Smith O'Brien has been in our opinion derogatory to his station in society and injurious to the character and interests of the Club'.[19] The meeting was duly held on 1 December and, perhaps surprisingly, merely decided to defer the matter to the next annual general meeting.[20] Meanwhile the Secretary was

---

* Club stories tend to be apocryphal: while its truth cannot be vouched for, it is nevertheless worth recounting the story of the young officer visiting the Oxford and Cambridge Club while the Guards' Club (at that time next door) was closed for cleaning. 'I say,' he drawled to the elderly gentleman hidden behind a newspaper, 'you fellows in the middle classes do yourselves well and no mistake!' The newspaper was lowered to disclose the Duke of Wellington.

instructed to write to Smith O'Brien, by now languishing in Dublin Gaol, apprising him of what had taken place.

When Smith O'Brien was told that his sentence had been commuted to transportation to Australia he was not placated and insisted that he would prefer to be hung, beheaded and quartered. This put the Government in a dilemma and a special bill had to be rushed through Parliament to deny him the option. He was duly transported, but not before he had written a letter resigning from the club. Some years later when all the fuss had died down he was pardoned and returned to live quietly in Ireland, where he died in 1864.

The New University Club

'Beyond the facts', observes a commentator in 1922, 'that the New University is the only 'Varsity club in St James's Street, that its frontage stands out in a prominent way, and that it is obviously a flourishing concern, there does not appear to be any particular reason (unless, of course, you be a member or a guest) for loitering at it.'[21]

But not so fast, for the New University is the third panel in our triptych of university clubs in London. Like the Oxford and Cambridge, it was founded, in 1864, to accommodate those awaiting election at the older clubs, at a meeting held at Willis's Rooms in King Street, St James's on 12 May.

The club found temporary premises in 57 and 58 St James's Street, on the corner of St James's Street and Bennet Street – a site occupied today by a motor showroom. Within ten months the Building sub-committee reported that an adjoining property, Nos 10 and 11 Arlington Street, had most conveniently become available, and suggested that a competent architect should be employed to inspect it as a site for a permanent club house with a lease of at least sixty years.[22] A few days later a special meeting of the general committee resolved to employ Alfred Waterhouse to inspect the site.[23]

Waterhouse went on to become a major Victorian architect, favouring the 'Gothic' school in the battle of the styles, with a *penchant* for unsympathetic materials such as blood-red brick and terracotta:* the Natural History Museum, St Paul's School (now demolished) and the Prudential Building in High Holborn bear his trademark. He had started his practice in Manchester where he won the competition for the Assize Court in a Venetian Gothic of which even Ruskin approved, and where he would go on to design Manchester Town Hall and Strangeways Prison, which was based on Bentham's Panopticon. But in 1865 he had only just begun practising in London in order to enter the Law Courts competition (won by Street), and the New University Club was among the very first of his London buildings. Though he later went on to work in Oxford (at Balliol) and to do unspeakable things to the view from King's Parade (Caius), he would at this stage of his career have been little known to the academic community. It seems highly probable that it was A. J. B. Beresford-Hope,† a firm advocate of the Gothic principle in art, who drew Waterhouse to the committee's attention: he certainly took the chair at the Extraordinary General Meeting in 1865 which approved the plans.[24]

In July 1865 Waterhouse reported on the possibility of a club house on the joint sites of 57 and 58 St James's Street and 10 and 11 Arlington Street. 'I beg to inform you that I have considered the question of building a new Club on the site of the present Club and Nos 10 and 11 Arlington Street, and I believe that the accommodation I will now describe may be obtained at a cost of £13,500 more or less.'‡[25] It was to consist of three floors, a mezzanine and a basement. The ground floor was to contain the entrance hall and staircases, with a morning room at the front, a coffee room, strangers' dining room, waiting room and serving room at the back: on the first floor there would be a drawing room (at the front), a card room, a library (over the coffee room) a

---

* Hence his nickname of 'Slaughterhouse'. Sir John Betjeman rated him the greatest English architect since Wren. Not everyone agrees.
† He became Member of Parliament for Cambridge University in 1868.
‡ As it transpired, more rather than less: the lowest tender received, from a Mr William Brass, was £18,242. Waterhouse's fee was £1,100. The contract was signed on 8 August 1866. To pay the cost the committee hoped the members would buy £15,000-worth of debentures. By May 1867 £13,490 had been raised in this way.

NEW UNIVERSITY CLUB. ST. JAMES'S STREET FRONT.——Mr. Waterhouse, Architect.

The NUC, 1868

committee room and a writing room: and on the second floor a smoking room (over the drawing room), a billiard room and a conservatory. The basement and mezzanine would house the kitchen, larders, servants' rooms, one or two dressing rooms and a bathroom. Waterhouse estimated that this would all prove large enough for a club of a thousand to 1,200 members.

The style was of course vaguely Gothic (a later writer refers to 'that vast-windowed, rather ecclesiastical, building'[26]): the St James's Street front was faced with Portland stone, with the arms of the various colleges on it, the Arlington Street side was white brick, with stone dressings. It was demolished just before the outbreak of the Second World War.

While the club house was being built the committee took a lease on No. 1 Savile Row as a temporary home. On 6 June 1868 the new house was ready and opened its doors. However, it seems the Arlington Street-St James's Street venue was not to everyone's entire satisfaction, for the Secretary was, within ten days of their return there, directed to write to the Commissioners of Police calling attention to the nuisance occasioned by organ-grinders and others in Arlington Street (the Police replied that it was not within their province to stop street music).[27]

Qualifications for membership were a little less restrictive than at the older clubs, in that all that was required was three terms' residence at either university or an honorary degree. The entrance fee was twenty guineas for the first 600 members, thereafter twenty-five guineas, and the annual subscription was six guineas, increased in 1867 to seven and in 1871 to eight. The original membership of 600 grew by 1865 to 800 and by 1876 to a thousand. One gains the impression that the average age may have been somewhat lower than at the older clubs. Fifty of the original 600 were clergy. There was a sprinkling of politicians, though far fewer than had been the case when the other clubs were founded: by now the politicians had their own clubs. Apart from Gladstone, none was of the first rank. The Law was well represented, as were the Universities: both A. V. Dicey, the constitutional historian and G. O. Trevelyan, the biographer and father of G. M. Trevelyan, a future Master of Trinity, Cambridge, were founder members.

Thus, by the mid-1860s there were no fewer than three Oxford and Cambridge clubs in London, with a total membership of over 3,000: in fact, roughly the same number of members as today, though it must be remembered that the universities were far smaller then. Bearing in mind the cost of joining, the fact that no concessions in subscription were made to country members and that many of them must rarely have visited London, it was a remarkable phenomenon.

Notes to Chapter I

1. E. Beresford Chancellor. *Memorials of St James's Street*, p. 157
2. All quoted in F. H. W. Sheppard (ed.). *Survey of London*, vol XXIX, Pt 1, p. 323
3. UUC AGMM, 8 May 1824
4. Charles Crawley. *Trinity Hall*, p. 121
5. Jonathan Gathorne-Hardy. *The Public School Phenomenon*, p. 47
6. Gathorne-Hardy. *Ibid.*, p. 37
7. Arthur Griffiths. *Clubs and Clubmen*, p. 122
8. *The Athenaeum*, p. 129
9. OC GCM, 17 May 1830
10. OC GCM, 1 June 1830
11. OC GCM, 17 June 1830
12. N. T. P. Murphy. *One Man's London*, pp. 256–65
13. OC GCM, 12 May and 23 June 1831
14. OC GCM, 26 April 1832
15. OC GCM, 10 April 1834
16. OC GCM, 17 April 1834
17. Quoted in Anthony Lejeune. *The Gentlemen's Clubs of London*, p. 183
18. OC GCM, 2 August 1848
19. OC GCM, 29 November 1848
20. OC GCM, 1 December 1848
21. Chancellor. *op. cit.*, p. 163
22. NUC GCM, 21 March 1865
23. NUC GCM, 29 March 1865
24. NUC EGMM, 17 July 1865
25. NUC EGMM, 17 July 1865
26. Chancellor. *op. cit.*, p. 163
27. NUC GCM, 16 June 1868

Chapter II

The Middle-Class Paradise

Gibbon placed his golden age of the ancient world, 'during which the condition of the human race was most happy and prosperous', between AD96 and AD180; between the death of Domitian and the accession of Commodus.[1] A more parochial historian of modern English society would be greatly tempted to place its golden age in the later Victorian and the Edwardian eras. Not just for the well-to-do but for a substantial section of middle-class society, it was a period of material prosperity and increasing assurance. As John Buchan recalled in his memoirs,

London at the turn of the Century had not yet lost her Georgian air ... Her great houses had not disappeared or become blocks of flats. In the summer she was a true city of pleasure, every window box gay with flowers, her streets full of splendid equipages, the Park a show ground for fine horses and handsome men and women ... Also Clubs were still in their hey-dey, their waiting lists were lengthy, membership of the right ones was a stage in a career ... Looking back, that time seems to me unbelievably secure and self-satisfied. The world was friendly and well-bred as I remember it, without the vulgarity and the worship of wealth which appeared with the new century.[2]

Only half the story, of course, for it was the era of Charles Booth's *Poverty* as well as of the Forsytes; but the age of the Forsytes is no less real for that. Once the depression of the first decade of Victoria's reign had passed, it had become a period of growing wealth, and one requiring a much larger ruling class than hitherto, in order to provide the country and the empire with officers, colonial and civil servants, judges and magistrates. For such as these (provided that they were not mainly dependent on land and agriculture for their income) life was sweet. In the 1890s and the early years of the twentieth century income tax was a shilling in the pound, death duties (only introduced in 1894) were 8%. Travel was cheap and easy and rents moderate: a house in St James's Place could be rented for two hundred pounds a year, and a staff to run it (consisting of cook, parlour maid and house maid) cost £64. Buchan was quite right to call this the hey-dey of the clubs; waiting lists were indeed lengthy. Since more members meant extra income, there was always a temptation to let the membership rise beyond the number originally contemplated. It had happened at Suffolk Street till by 1833 there were complaints from members at the Annual General Meeting that the place was overcrowded, particularly in the coffee room. They resolved to reduce members to the original thousand – a lengthy process not finally achieved till 1846. Meanwhile the waiting lists grew and grew: by 1861 there were 400 candidates awaiting election; by 1878, 506, and by 1885, 692.[3] Since the vacancies occurring each year rarely exceeded twenty, a candidate might well have a ten-year wait, even allowing for the fact that some on the list would tire of waiting and join one of the other four Oxford and Cambridge Clubs flourishing at that date.

However, once his turn came – and for an Oxford man it always took a little longer since the Oxford waiting list was for some reason always lengthier than the Cambridge one – the ordeal of the ballot box was not nearly so severe as at some clubs. Ten votes were needed, and one black ball in ten was sufficient to exclude. Though many names in the candidates' books are marked 'not elected', this does not mean necessarily that they had been blackballed, but simply that for one reason or another they had withdrawn their candidacy. For some, no doubt, it was the difficulty of finding the formidable entrance fee, which by 1891 at the Oxford and Cambridge Club was forty guineas – that is, about £1,500 in today's money.

These hurdles surmounted, the new member could begin to enjoy for the comparatively modest annual subscription of eight guineas the pleasures of a club of which contemporaries spoke highly.* The cost of doing so was, likewise, modest. The principles of club finance were quite simple: the initial expense of building and equipping the club house was defrayed from the entrance fees of the original members, and those paid by subsequent members would cover the cost of maintenance and refurbishment. Other overheads such as rent and wages were to be met from subscriptions which would from time to time have to be adjusted. The charges for food and drink merely had to break even. As a contemporary writer explained:

The object of these associations is to possess an establishment, with all domestic necessities, whereby the members are provided with breakfasts, dinners, etc., at the cost of the respective articles. The wines are also laid in of the best qualities, and in large quantities, and are furnished to the members at the original prices. Hence the accommodation and advantages they afford to single gentlemen, and to those who occasionally visit the metropolis, are very considerable, and admission is consequently eagerly sought for.[4]

Both at Suffolk Street and in Pall Mall, therefore, a member could dine well for extraordinarily little: in 1882 the committee at the former club resolved 'That a Club dinner be served at 3/6d per head, consisting of soup, fish, joint or plain entrée, small entrée or sweet, including table money'. In the following year the committee at the latter club went one better and threw in an extra course (entrée *and* joint) for the same price. Both clubs provided beer or porter and bread free to members.[5] The story that at Suffolk Street a member was seen to complete his meal with a bowl of soup because he had not at first noticed it was on the *table d'hôte* and he wanted his money's-worth sounds about as reliable as most club anecdotes, but it is quite true that at the Oxford and Cambridge the Steward was directed 'that no extra charge should be made for a second portion of any dish of the Club Dinner for the day, and that 6d should be returned to Mr C. A. Reeve.[6]

Both clubs quickly acquired renowned cellars, as notable for their quality as for their size. According to T. H. S. Escott,

---

* 'Creature comforts are not neglected; the cellar at the Oxford and Cambridge is well stocked and maintained, and the cook is a *cordon bleu.*' A. G. F. Griffiths. *Clubs and Clubmen.*

The chief baron of the Exchequer, both as Sir James Scarlett and
Lord Abinger, Sir John Johnstone, R. Bell, Lord Melbourne's
younger brother, George Lamb, and his private secretary, T. Young,
at the United University, not only had a genius in wine judgement
amounting almost to an instinct, but seemed to know intuitively
where new and priceless acquisitions for their club cellars from time
to time might be found.[7]

Through the good offices of the British consuls in Cadiz and
Bordeaux, the wine committee was able to import its own butts
of sherry and claret which were then stored in bond until needed
in a cellar rented at St Katherine's Dock. Under the guidance of
Sir John Mowbray, MP, its chairman, the wine committee at the
Oxford and Cambridge Club quickly acquired for the cellars of
its new club house an astonishing quantity of wine: their report
on stocks in 1841 listed four butts of sherry and five pipes of port
(in the wood) as well as over a thousand dozen bottles of port,
five hundred dozen of sherry, 1,039 of claret and 365 of Madeira.
This was besides two thousand bottles and 1,100 pints of various
wines for immediate consumption in the dispense cellar.

Unlike the political clubs such as the Carlton, the Reform and
the National Liberal, which sought to influence the course of
events in the world outside, the university clubs have tended to
be places for getting away from them. Until war came in 1914
references to them in the clubs' records are few and far between:
the only purely political event marked by any of the clubs was in
1832 when the committee at Suffolk Street 'Anticipating the
probability of an Illumination taking place suddenly on the Reform Bill being passed – Ordered that Lamps be used if time
permit. Device Crown and an R with Laurel Branches'.[8] Thirty
years later they decided to order 'Some cheap maps of the seat of
War in America', and in 1873 the New University Club likewise
ordered a 'Map of the Ashantee War to be got'.[9] During the Boer
War they agreed that used packs of cards should be sent for
soldiers proceeding to South Africa and the UUC voted to send
them its old newspapers. At the Oxford and Cambridge Club it
had been decided in 1839, rather daringly, to take in the Chartist
newspaper: in 1851 the club bought an illustrated catalogue of the

Bin		Bot.	Pt.	½-Pt.	
22	Allan Vint 1846	5/-	2/6	1/3	PORT.
22	Barnes Vint 1847	5/-	2/6	1/3	SHERRY.
24	Bull Old & Dry	7/6	3/9		
41	Christopher Vint 1820	21/-			CLARET.
107	D° Vint 1833	14/-			BURGUNDY.
20	D° Vint 1836	11/-			MADEIRA.
106	Claridge Vint 1846	10/6			
89	D° „ 1853	8/-			CHAMPAGNE.
81	Kingston Vint 1834	10/6			HOCK.
82	Tanqueray Old & Dry	9/6			MOSELLE.
114	Day Vint 1847	5/-	2/6	1/3	
20	Christopher Vint 1858	4/-	2/-	1/-	SAUTERNE.
					BARSAC.
					CHABLIS.

Extract from the O&C wine list, 1870

Great Exhibition in Hyde Park. But in 1900, when a letter from Mr Jasper More MP suggested a dinner in the club 'to celebrate the relief of Ladysmith', the committee, perhaps wisely, declined 'and were strongly of opinion that it would be premature at the present time even to consider the question of any festivities in the Club, in connection with the war'.[10]

Public ceremonial occasions, however, were a quite different matter: in company with many other clubs, especially those fortunate enough to have premises overlooking the processional routes of Piccadilly, St James's Street and Pall Mall, the university clubs celebrated royal birthdays, coronations and jubilees with an 'Illumination'. In 1831, though still tucked away in Sir John Beckett's house in St James's Square, the Oxford and Cambridge decided to illuminate the club house for William IV's coronation – which meant in practice putting a row of oil lamps on the balcony facing St James's Square and lighting flambeaux along the King Street side. The United University did likewise, arranging for the club house to be opened at 7 a.m. for the benefit of members attending the coronation. Seven years later, for Queen Victoria's coronation, both clubs went further and, possibly for the first time, allowed ladies into the club for the event. The Oxford and Cambridge, now installed in their new club house in Pall Mall, ordered a gas design for illumination on Coronation night and even hired a band. At Suffolk Street the three hundred ladies admitted were to be provided with a cold collation, 'on a liberal but not extravagant scale'.[11]

There might well have been a fifty-year wait before another royal occasion, in the form of Victoria's Golden Jubilee, presented the ladies with a further opportunity to explore the mysteries of their husbands' clubs, but when the Duke of Wellington died in 1852 the committee of the Oxford and Cambridge met specially to make arrangements for the funeral of their most famous member. Scaffolding was to be erected to make a stand to hold four hundred people. Ladies were to be admitted; tickets were to cost a guinea. On 18 November the funeral procession took exactly two hours to pass through Pall Mall (there had been a hitch when the enormously heavy funeral coach had got stuck

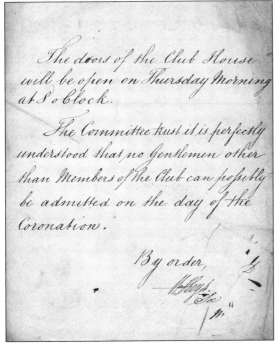

Arrangements for the coronation of Queen Victoria

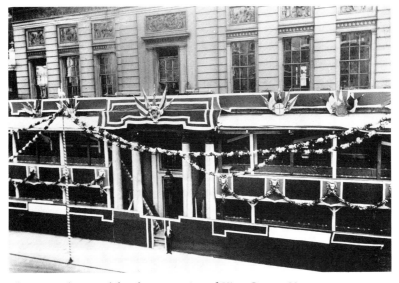

The O&C decorated for the coronation of King George V, 1911

in the Mall). 'The front balconies of the Oxford and Cambridge Club were tastefully hung with black cloth, festooned with silver lace, the letter "W" enclosed in laurel wreaths, being inserted in temporary hatchments.'[12] The Oxford and Cambridge in particular seems to have acquired at this period a taste for such affairs: the visit of the King of Sardinia to London in 1855, the return of the Guards to London in 1856 (presumably from the Crimea) and the wedding of the Princess Royal in 1858 all provided opportunities for illuminations and for the Prince of Wales's wedding in 1863 they really pushed the boat out. * But no further opportunities were to present themselves until the Queen's golden and diamond jubilees in 1887 and 1897, followed by Edward VII's and George V's coronations in 1901 and 1911.

The intervening years, however, were not devoid of excitement. In October 1887 a member at Suffolk Street made the following entry in the club suggestion book: 'If the Mob are much longer allowed as they have for the last ten days to hold their meetings in Trafalgar Square I venture to suggest that the unfortunate Policemen who guard the Club and its neighbourhood be once a day supplied with refreshments such as hot coffee and sandwiches at the direction of the Committee'. What was happening? It was forty years since the Duke of Wellington, even then in his seventy-ninth year but still Commander-in-Chief, had brought troops to key points in London and enrolled hundreds of special constables in case the Chartists marched on Westminster with their monster petition. Since that time, greater prosperity and social reform had dulled people's fears that the West End might ever again be invaded by the East End. Yet on 8 February 1886 ('Black Monday'), probably because of a sharp rise in the number of unemployed, the Social Democratic Federation and various other groups, such as the Fair Trade League, seized the chance to organise meetings, often in Trafalgar Square. Afterwards, with John Burns in the lead waving a red flag, a considerable crowd marched down Pall Mall. There was jeering

---

* Platforms to be erected, ladies admitted, luncheon to be prepared for 500 (members 5/-, ladies 1 guinea, to include lunch, sherry and claret: champagne extra, 6/- a bottle or 3/- a pint).

from the Reform Club and the marchers retaliated by smashing the windows of several clubs (including the Oxford and Cambridge and the New University Club). On reaching Piccadilly the crowd looted a number of shops on their way to Hyde Park. It all resulted in two hundred claims for damages amounting to £11,000 and four of those who had spoken at the meeting, including John Burns and H. M. Hyndman, being prosecuted for sedition.*

A further result was that the Commissioner of Police (Sir Charles Warren) tried to put an end to the use of Trafalgar Square for political meetings; but the more the police interfered, the larger the meetings became. It was to these events that the member writing in the Suffolk Street Suggestion Book was alluding. Matters finally came to a head on 13 November 1887 ('Bloody Sunday') when Warren banned outright a meeting called to demand the release of William O'Brien MP and the organisers sought to baffle the police by approaching the Square from all sides simultaneously. Some were dispersed by baton charges but many succeeded in reaching the Square. So serious did matters become that the police had to be reinforced by the Foot Guards and Life Guards, and it was the latter with their horses who eventually cleared the Square. No shots were fired, but two died of injuries and there were over a hundred casualties.

Times improved and there was no sequel, but the Oxford and Cambridge Club made a claim under the Metropolitan Police (Compensation) Act of 1886 for the windows smashed in the Black Monday riot. In 1887 the Guards' Club next door suggested a subscription to provide the police on duty with refreshments. The committee did not agree, but nevertheless sent a cheque to Sir Charles Warren for fifty pounds.[13] At Suffolk Street a subscription by members raised £33–6s.[14] Pall Mall has seen

---

* Hyndman was the founder of the Social Democratic Federation, the only overtly Marxist organisation of British socialists at that time. He had also been a founder member of the New University Club, from which he had recently been expelled, presumably for his political activities (the minute book for the period has unfortunately not survived). The prosecution failed: Burns, Hyndman and the rest were found not guilty. But one yearns to know whether Hyndman had taken revenge for his expulsion by inciting the mob to smash the windows of his former club.

nothing like it since, though Trafalgar Square saw violence enough during the Poll Tax riot in 1990. Fortunately for the clubs, the rioters dispersed in other directions, taking their toll of destruction as they went.

Though the names and attainments of most of the Victorian and Edwardian members have inevitably faded into the fog of history, the members' lists and candidates' books continue to read like a roll-call of the Great and the Good or of those who would become such with the passing of time. The component elements did not vary greatly since the time the clubs were founded. The great flocks of clergy were headed by three Archbishops of Canterbury: Howley, who had been Regius Professor of Divinity at Oxford and who, as Archbishop, had with the Lord Chamberlain broken the news to Princess Victoria at Kensington Palace that William IV was dead; Tait, who had been Headmaster of Rugby and became Archbishop in 1868; and Temple, also a Headmaster of Rugby, who was Archbishop from 1886 to 1902. The first belonged in Suffolk Street, while the others were members of the Oxford and Cambridge, which seems to have taken over as the club for headmasters where the United University left off: Kynaston (High Master of St Paul's) was a Suffolk Street member but George Moberly (Headmaster of Winchester and later Bishop of Salisbury), Bertram Pollock* and William Vaughan (both Masters of Wellington, the latter going on to be Headmaster of Rugby in 1921), William Rutherford (Head Master of Westminster) and Frederick Walker (High Master first at Manchester Grammar School and then of St Paul's) – all these

---

* Harold Nicolson, who did not much enjoy his schooldays at Wellington, and was in fact deleted from the list of Old Wellingtonians for writing about it in *Some People* (though they eventually reinstated him as a governor), nevertheless venerated Pollock, who went on to become Bishop of Norwich: 'Dr Pollock, for his part, appeared to devote his energies to destroying all the educational convictions which we had hitherto absorbed: he taught us that the mere avoidance of howlers was a means only and not an end: he taught us that the greater proportion of classical literature as it figured in the school curriculum was not only dull but silly: that the really jolly bits were yet to come: he taught us that life was more than scholarship, and literature more than books: he taught us to feel and even to think, for ourselves.' (*Some People*, Constable 1930 ed., p. 45).

were at the Oxford and Cambridge.

Legal luminaries bulk so large in the membership lists of all three clubs that it would be tedious to recite them: Suffolk Street in particular was able, year after year, to call upon an almost unending procession of Lord Chief Justices, Masters of the Rolls, Lords of Appeal and High Court Judges to chair its general meetings. Many years after the event, when he was chairing the Annual General Meeting in 1932, Mr Justice Avory recalled the occasion in 1905 when the club feared that it could not stay in Suffolk Street since that would involve taking a new lease on the whole block between Suffolk Street and Whitcomb Street. A Special Committee had even been set up to find an alternative and they had lighted on No. 11 St James's Square, a freehold, which they undertook to purchase. However, when the Crown Commissioners relented and allowed the club to remain on its existing Suffolk Street site and the Special Committee recommended doing that, the owner of the St James's Square site

began threatening an action against us for specific performance of our offer of purchase of the house in St James's Square. Needless to say we repudiated any liability, and we were told afterwards that the solicitor to the owner of the House had advised his client as the Sub-Committee consisted of the Lord Chief Justice, a Lord of Appeal, a Metropolitan Magistrate and a Treasury Counsel, not to go to law.[15]

Clearly, the legal profession has its uses but, as will shortly be seen, it was a county court judge who brought about one of the greatest crises in the history of the Oxford and Cambridge Club, which could well have resulted in the collapse not just of that club but of many others as well.

Academics' bubble reputations usually last only till their research is superseded, but some are still remembered. At the Oxford and Cambridge Club, for example, Henry Latham,* fellow, Senior Tutor and subsequently Master of Trinity Hall over half a century, twice served on the committee in the 1880s and 1890s: he

---

* Innovators are not universally loved, but Latham endeared himself to generations of undergraduates. He was unable to pronounce the letter R ('Here you must either wead or wide or wow'), and became forgetful, once in chapel leading off the Creed 'I believe – in Pontius Pilate [pause] no, I don't!'

transformed the Hall from being an exclusively legal college with thirty-nine undergraduate into one of the leaders among the smaller colleges.[16] The economist, Nassau Senior, was the first Professor of Political Economy at Oxford and served on many if not most of the great reforming Royal Commissions of the mid-nineteenth century. Appropriately, the club enlisted his services as its auditor. F. W. Maitland, Downing Professor of Law at Cambridge, was founder of the Selden Society. He was a close friend and the biographer of Sir Leslie Stephen, another member, who was designer and first editor (1882–91)of the *Dictionary of National Biography*, and was the father of Vanessa Bell and Virginia Woolf. The historian Sir Charles Grant Robertson tutored the future Edward VIII during his time at Oxford. He was a Fellow of All Souls and later Principal and Vice-Chancellor of Birmingham University: he is best remembered for his biography of Bismarck.

It is slightly disappointing though not unexpected that the clubs in this period numbered among their members no writers of any stature: perhaps such as would have been eligible preferred the more bohemian atmosphere at the Garrick or the Savile or the Athenaeum. Of such minor literary figures as did belong, probably only Alexander Kinglake, author of *Eothen*, is still in print. W. M. Praed, a very minor poet and a member at Suffolk Street, does make *The Oxford Dictionary of Quotations* with a few unmemorable lines, but cannot have been much read for a long time. George Venables had been at Charterhouse with W. M. Thackeray, whose nose he broke in a fight there: he is said to be the original of George Warrington in *Pendennis* and is better remembered for that than for anything he wrote himself. One member at the Oxford and Cambridge, Matthew Higgins, had a talent for vivid descriptive writing: he witnessed at first hand the horrors of the Irish famine in the 1840s and described them eloquently in a letter to *The Times*. He was in fact an inveterate writer of letters to that newspaper under a variety of signatures – 'Civilian', 'Paterfamilias', 'Mother of Six'. According to his biographer in the *DNB*, his talents were first revealed to him through the impression he made on the committee of the club by a letter complaining of a bad dinner he had drafted for a friend.

On the fringes of both literature and politics was Richard Monckton Milnes (created first Baron Houghton).* Though his achievements in both fields were negligible, he was one of those figures who crop up in almost every aspect of Victorian public life. A member of both the Oxford and Cambridge and the New University Club, he knew practically everyone who was anyone. He was present at every great social gathering and was a famous after-dinner speaker. He was a fellow of the Royal Society, Secretary for foreign correspondence at the Royal Academy and succeeded Carlyle as president of the London Library. Another who also combined literature and politics was Augustine Birrell, another member of the New University Club. Good-natured but rather indolent, he served as President of the Board of Education in Campbell-Bannerman's ministry and as Chief Secretary for Ireland under Asquith, a post from which he eventually resigned for having failed completely to foresee the Dublin Easter Rising in 1916.

For reasons already given, politicians were not so numerous in later Victorian and Edwardian times as they had been in the earlier days of the clubs, but there were always some. A. W. Peel, the Speaker of the House of Commons who ruled in 1886 that Charles Bradlaugh must be allowed to take his seat after having been thrice re-elected, was a member at Suffolk Street, where he was made a trustee in the same year. Spencer Walpole, Home Secretary in Derby's first and second ministries, was another, as was Austin Chamberlain, twice Chancellor of the Exchequer and Foreign Secretary from 1924 to 1929. Both served a stint on the committee, the latter becoming a trustee in 1913. The unfortunate Sir Charles Dilke, driven from political office when he was cited as co-respondent in a divorce case in 1886, was a member at the New University Club; whether he also had to resign from his club is not clear. Another member there was Lord Milner, more statesman than politician, the star product of Jowett's Balliol.

---

* He is said to have been the original of Mr Vavasour in Disraeli's *Tancred* and of Mr Bertie Tremaine in *Endymion*.

Oxford finally awarded him its accolade by making him Chancellor just one month before he died.

The political connection at the Oxford and Cambridge Club was remarkably strong, notwithstanding the fact that the overall number of MPs who were members was declining. It is interesting to note that of the twenty-three cabinets covering the reigns of Victoria and Edward VII, only four did not contain at least one member of the club.* Apart from three Prime Ministers (Palmerston, Gladstone and Campbell-Bannerman), they included Wellington (Cabinet Minister without office in Peel's second cabinet), Sidney Herbert (Secretary at War in 1852, Secretary for the Colonies in 1855 and Secretary for War in 1859), Edward (later Viscount) Cardwell (Chief Secretary for Ireland in 1859 and Secretary for War in 1868), Gathorne Hardy (Lord Cranbrook) (Secretary for War in 1874 and Lord President in 1885), Vernon Harcourt (Home Secretary from 1880 to 1885 and Chancellor of the Exchequer in 1886 and again from 1892 to 1895) and Sir Edward Grey (Foreign Secretary first under Campbell-Bannerman and then under Asquith). Other notables were William Court Gulley (Viscount Selby) who became Speaker of the Commons in 1898 and holds the distinction of having named no fewer than twenty-three members in one afternoon in 1901, and Sir John Mowbray, MP for Oxford University from 1868 to 1899. He became Father of the House in the year before he died.†

All three Prime Ministers who were members of the Oxford and Cambridge took an active interest in the club's affairs. Palmerston had, of course, presided at the founding meeting and served on the committee (albeit not as a very frequent attender of its meetings) till he left it by rotation in 1834. Campbell-Bannerman served on the committee in 1908 and was also a trustee. By far the most active, though, was Gladstone. He joined all three clubs. At Suffolk Street he put up for membership in January, 1832, proposed by Sir Robert Inglis, the Member of

* These were Derby's first and second ministries (1852 and 1858–59), Salisbury's third (1895–1902) and Balfour's first (1902–05). In each except for Salisbury's, however, the United University filled the gap.
† His portrait hangs in the members' bar.

Parliament for Oxford University, and remained a Member there until he died. He was elected to the committee in 1837 and again in 1858 after he had resigned as Chancellor of the Exchequer in Palmerston's first cabinet, and remained on it till 1861 even though he became Chancellor again in Palmerston's second cabinet in June 1859, though the minutes show that he only attended five meetings. At the AGM in 1863 it was he who proposed that the Prince of Wales be made an honorary member, and in 1874 did likewise for Prince Leopold: since the Prince was not 'duly qualified' and hence was not really eligible, this was only achieved by the somewhat cavalier device of calling a special meeting and passing a resolution to suspend the club rules while the election was carried out. Gladstone was elected to the Oxford and Cambridge Club in 1833, again proposed by Sir Robert Inglis. Here also he served on the committee from 1834 to 1838. His main recorded contribution was to arrange in 1837 for a pew to be rented at the chapel in York Street so that the club servants could attend on Sundays.* For reasons unknown, he withdrew from the club in 1842, but joined the New University Club in 1864 or 1865, when he was again Chancellor of the Exchequer in Palmerston's second ministry.

In Regency times young gentlemen had displayed their physical prowess in the hunting field or perhaps with the four-in-hand or even in the prize-ring. Within that tradition falls the sad case of Hayes St Leger, fourth Viscount Doneraile, a member of the Oxford and Cambridge and an MFH in Ireland who died in 1887 from hydrophobia caused by a bite from a fox. As the cult of athleticism and organised games spread in Victorian times through the public schools and the universities it is not surprising to find it reflected in the achievements of club members, all carefully and proudly recorded for posterity by the club librarian. Among them was the Rt Reverend Charles Wordsworth, chief founder of the inter-university cricket match and boat race. The Reverend Thomas Staniforth had rowed for Oxford in the first

---

* This was later changed to St Philip's, Regent Street. Whether because the club servants were less than appreciative of his concern for their spiritual welfare or for some other reason, the practice was discontinued in 1858.

boat race in 1829: he lived to dine with the crews in Freemasons' Hall in 1881 at a banquet to commemorate the fiftieth anniversary. Another member, Leonard Gaskell Pike, rowed for Cambridge in 1877, the year of the dead heat. Yet another, John George Wilson, had been among the four who, in 1870, ran the hundred yards flat in ten seconds.

According to Charles Graves it was difficult before the First World War for solicitors and doctors to join a good club because old members disliked the idea of hobnobbing with people who knew too much about their insides and private affairs.[17] One might expect the same to have held for bankers: however, it seems unlikely that the university clubs' banker members were of the kind that would have been much interested in members' affairs, for David Powell at the Oxford and Cambridge was Governor of the Bank of England, Lord Cunliffe at the New University was its manager and Samuel Jones Loyd (Lord Overstone) at Suffolk Street, a leading promoter of the Great Exhibition, was one of the richest men in England and died worth two million pounds.

Writing in 1907, Arthur Griffiths makes the point that 'the most curious feature in club ethics is the aloofness of detachment of its members, generally, from the conduct or its concerns; they throw all responsibility upon the committee, and claim only to find fault'.[18] This placed a heavy burden on the committees and more particularly since, though they met far more frequently than today but were usually less well attended, upon the chairmen. Yet, curiously, it was many years before the United University ever seems to have had a proper chairman: whenever the committee met, one of its number would take the chair and it was seldom the same person for two meetings running. For a short period in the 1840s it did become the practice for one member to do so on a fairly regular basis, and on one occasion he did actually sign himself as 'J. Geo. Brett, Chairman'; but it did not last for long. It was not until 1888 that a proposal to appoint a chairman (and two vice-chairmen) was adopted and E. H. Pember, QC was elected for a period of one year.[19] At the Oxford and

Cambridge they went almost to the opposite extreme: The Reverend Montague Taylor* became Chairman in 1863 and although he had to go off the committee by rotation from time to time in conformity with the club rules, he was re-elected again and again. By the time of his death in 1896 he had served thirty years on the committee, fifteen of them as Chairman.

With or without a chairman, the members at Suffolk Street certainly exercised their claim to find fault. At each weekly meeting the committee was usually subjected to a string of letters from members, only a few of which were complimentary, and the surviving Suggestion Book, covering the years from 1881 to 1939, is a social document of the greatest human interest concerning the quirks and foibles of members down the years. Probably every club has a member or two whose chief recreation or even occupation it is to find fault. Among the most persistent and vigorous of these at Suffolk Street, and a club character in his own right, was Mr J. H. Noyes, Junior. His name first comes to light in the AGM Minutes for 1864 when he dominated the meeting with two denunciations of the committee for the 'extortionate' prices in the coffee room and for their general incompetence. This performance was repeated at the 1865, 1866 and 1867 AGMs – though on the last occasion the other members present rallied to the defence of the committee and – temporarily – silenced him. By 1870 the committee had clearly had enough of him and in one of the most heated AGMs in the club's history it was resolved that Mr Noyes was 'deserving of grave censure on three offences – 1. Failing to pay for a mutton chop, 2. Failing to pay for the use of the billiard room, and 3. Failing to pay for tearing the cloth'[20] but really, one suspects, for having made himself such a nuisance. Undeterred, Mr Noyes returned to the attack in the following year: at an Extraordinary General Meeting called in 1871 to discuss an extension to the club house he denounced the committee for their extravagance, though on the particular issue he chose he had unfortunately got his facts wrong. He was objecting to the

---

* About whom nothing further is discoverable apart from the fact that he had been an undergraduate at Brasenose. His portrait (paid for by members) hangs in the coffee room.

Some nineteenth-century members of the O&C: Mr James Clay, MP;
Rev. Montague J. Taylor; Sir J. E. Eardley Wilmot, Bart; Mr Thomas Price;
Lord Houghton; Rt Hon. J. R. Mowbray, MP; Mr G. Leveson Gower MP;
Rev. G. E. Prescott

Lord Houghton

Right Hon.ᵇˡᵉ J. R. Mowbray M.P.

Mr. G. Leveson Gower M.P.

Rev.ᵈ G. E. Prescott.

item of Sunlights (a patent gas lighting device)

that Gas not only made the Coffee Room too hot but greatly discoloured it, as evidenced by the present condition of the room, but on being reminded by Mr M. Bere that there was no gas in the Coffee Room, he resumed his seat.[21]

By 1874 the committee really had had enough of him: not only had he been bouncing cheques at the Oxford and Cambridge and New University Clubs when they offered the UUC hospitality in the summer: he had now presented the committee with an opening by spending a whole night in the club. They pounced, and an Extraordinary General Meeting was called for 22 June which resolved by a majority of 121 votes to 41 'that the name of Mr J. Herbert Noyes, Junior be removed from the Club'. 'Mr Noyes Jnr then said', then minutes continue, 'that the proceedings of that Meeting would be brought before the Judges of the land, and that those who had taken part in it would go down to their graves with it on their consciences.'[22]

Even now the committee had not heard the last of him: they offered to return his year's subscription but he refused to accept it: a few days later he wrote, announcing his intention of continuing to use the club. The committee replied that if he did, he would be ejected with as little violence as possible. He came, and was refused admittance by the Hall Porter. In December 1875 he again visited the club and abused a member. The committee told him that if he came again, the police could be called. In 1877 he again wrote, threatening to start legal proceedings to enforce his right to membership. Yet again in 1878 Mr Noyes visited the club and was apparently ejected, for a couple of months later his solicitor wrote to say that an assault had been committed on Mr Noyes by the Hall Porter. The committee denied assault and, no doubt thankfully, this was the last they heard of him. Mr Noyes was clearly a wag: he simply went too far.

In the more robust days of the Regency, heavy drinking and high stakes had often been the hallmarks if not the *raison d'être* of club life. By Victorian times the bounds of acceptable behaviour had altered, and what might once have excited no comment in

White's or Brooks's was regarded as scandalous in the new middle-class clubs. When, for example, one member of the Oxford and Cambridge Club in 1865 overdid things one evening, the committee took a most serious view and delivered (*via* the Secretary) a stinging rebuke:

Sir,
The Committee of the Oxford and Cambridge Club have the painful duty of informing you that a complaint has been made to them by several members of the Club that on the Evening of Monday the 13th inst of this month you were the cause of great annoyance to them in the coffee room, that you were intoxicated and acted with great violence, 1st in the Coffee room by addressing Members in an improper manner and by throwing a decanter into the fire place – and secondly in the Hall by presenting a drawn sword stick at the Night porter, such conduct being derogatory to your station in society, and injurious to the character and interests of the Club. The Committee therefore to their great regret are compelled to request you to give them any explanation you may think fit and to state whether you propose any course that may obviate the painful necessity they are under by rule 52 * of calling a General Meeting of the Club to consider the propriety of removing your name from the list of members.

By order of the Committee
W. H. Thomas
Secy.[23]

(He resigned without more ado).

Interesting, because it exemplifies the change in moral outlooks, was another incident which occurred a few years later at the same club in 1873. At a meeting on 10 October a Mr W. Marshall, a member of the committee, announced that he proposed to bring before it a serious charge against a young member called Mr Horace Browne. There was very few committee members present so the matter was deferred to a future meeting,

---

* Rule 52 stipulated that if the committee or twenty-five members think that 'the conduct of any member, either in or out of the club, shall be derogatory to his station in society, or injurious to the character and interests of the club, he shall be subject to expulsion' if two-thirds of a general meeting so decide.

but eventually a Special General Meeting of the club was convened to investigate the charge against Mr Browne under Rule 52. It transpired that Marshall and Browne had been playing cards (whist, presumably) for high stakes: in the course of the evening Browne lost to Marshall £5,491, which he could not pay. That was reprehensible no doubt, and in fact Browne resigned from the club; but the committee took the view that it was the elder man's conduct rather than Browne's which was injurious to the club, being directly in contravention of club rules about gambling, and he was called upon either to resign or to appear before an Extraordinary General Meeting under Rule 52. Marshall refused to resign, and when the meeting was duly held in February 1874, with the Solicitor-General in the chair, they voted to expel Marshall by a majority of 163 to 48.

Compared with what was to come later, inflation in the years before 1914 was not a serious problem for club finances. Nevertheless, it had been found necessary from time to time to increase subscriptions slightly. At the Oxford and Cambridge Club they had been raised in 1832 from five guineas to six, in 1867 from six to seven and in 1881 from seven to eight, after which they remained static for the next twenty years. In April 1902 the committee recommended to the Annual General Meeting that, to meet rising overheads, it would be prudent to raise the subscription from eight guineas to nine – a proposal to which the meeting assented by the necessary majority. One member, though, – Sir Richard Harington, a county court judge who had been a member of the club since 1886 – did not agree, arguing that whatever rate they might set for future members, neither the committee nor the Annual General Meeting had the power to alter the subscription, as set out in the rules, for existing members. He therefore refused to pay the extra guinea. A correspondence ensued between the Secretary (on behalf of the Committee) and Judge Harington, lasting several months. The committee, feeling sure of their ground, refused to budge, and rejected Harington's various proposals that the matter should be referred to Mr Justice Buckley, a member of the club, to learned counsel for arbitration or to one or more of three eminent judges who were members of the club (Lord Davey, Sir Ford North and Mr Justice Buckley) for their opinion.

By late November the dispute had become a pamphlet war, a printed circular being placed before the committee regarding the legality of the increased subscription, signed by Harington and three other members. The committee, sticking to their guns, replied in kind. When January 1903 arrived (the date at which the increased subscriptions fell due), the committee refused to accept cheques for less than nine guineas, and resolved 'That the Solicitor of the Club be instructed to enter an appearance to any legal proceedings which Sir R. Harington or his associates may institute against the Club or the Committee'.[24] At their next meeting the committee received a further batch of letters from members (eventually amounting to forty-two) protesting at the increased subscription, together with one from Harington saying that he proposed to litigate. The committee instructed the club solicitor to retain R. B. Haldane KC as leading counsel with R. V. Parker as junior.

The case of Harington *v.* Sendall came before Mr Justice Joyce on 3 and 4 March. It took the form of a motion by the plaintiff for an interlocutory injunction to restrain the defendants (the committee) from interfering with the enjoyment by the plaintiff of the benefits and privileges of the club, and from posting up the plaintiff's name as that of a member in default with his subscription, and from erasing the plaintiff's name from the list of members.

Counsel for the plaintiff argued that when he had joined the club, the rules stipulated that the annual subscription was eight guineas, and that the rules contained no provision for alteration or amendment. That being the case, the members had no inherent power to alter their rules so as to expel one of its members for non-payment of the additional guinea.

For the defendant, counsel argued that if the rules constituted a fundamental contract which any one member could prevent the majority from altering, then social clubs could not be carried on at all. If, for example, a majority of members at a general meeting decided that the club house should be enlarged, that would certainly involve an increase in expenditure. It would be unreasonable to hold that, although the majority of members could direct the committee to incur the increased expenditure, they had not also the power to raise the subscription to meet that increased expenditure. Further, it was argued, the plaintiff had never objected to any previous exercise of the power of the General Meeting to alter the rules, and so was precluded by acquiescence from raising any objection in the present instance.

The trial judge, however, took the view that as the rules, unfortunately in his view, contained no provision for the making of amendments or alterations from time to time, the majority of members had no power to alter the terms and constitution of the club as they thought fit. Just because the plaintiff had acquiesced in certain alterations of a minor character on previous occasions, this did not preclude him from insisting on his right to do so when a case arose in which his pecuniary interests were directly and materially affected. Though clearly not in sympathy with the plaintiff, the judge concluded,

Upon the whole case, then, I have not to consider the reasonableness or otherwise of what was proposed by the committee or approved by the general meeting, nor have I to consider the propriety or otherwise of the course taken by the dissentient minority under the circumstances of this case; but if the plaintiff insists upon it, I am compelled to come to the conclusion that he is entitled to the injunction which he seeks.[25]

So important was this judgment to the future of the Oxford and Cambridge (and indeed many another) club that counsel's opinion was that the committee should proceed with an appeal. Wisely, as it transpired, the committee resolved to defer a decision until they had put the matter before an Extraordinary General Meeting (several members had written against appealing, one suggesting that the committee, not the club, should pay the expense). When the EGM was held on 24 March, it voted (100 to 214) against appealing.

Harington had won his point and the club had to pay his costs, amounting to £80-10s. He neither resigned nor paid the increased subscription but simply went on paying at the old rate until his death, as did a number of other members. If he had intentionally set out to bring about the demise of his own club he could not have done it more thoroughly. Perhaps the satisfaction to the legal mind of scoring a legal point outweighed the consequences.

In this extremely messy situation, all the committee could do was to pick up the bits as best they could. They circularised members asking them to sign a form of assent to the one guinea increase in subscription (in fact 1,107 out of 1,171 members had already paid up in January without protest). At the AGM in May 1904, so as to overcome the Harington problem, a new rule (53) was added: 'New Rules, or repeal or alteration of existing Rules, may from time to time be made subject to the following conditions . . .'. These were, first, that two-thirds of the members present and voting must assent: second, that twenty-one days' notice of any change must be given; third – and least satisfactorily – that this rule did not apply to members elected prior to 18 May 1904.[26] All members were then circularised with a form of consent to be bound by Rule 53: by July only 754 had assented, but only 21 had actually dissented.

Members at the United University had never been entirely content with their club house in Suffolk Street. Handsome though Wilkins's design had been, the building simply was not big enough. In 1828, within four years of its completion, the committee was beginning to receive complaints of overcrowding and at the Annual General Meeting a motion, proposed by the Reverend W. F. Baylay and seconded by Dr James Franck (both members of the committee), suggested 'that authority be given to the Committee to take such measures as they may deem expedient for the building of a New Club House'.[27] At the next AGM the committee reported:

The Committee beg leave to state that in pursuance of the determination of the last General Meeting they proceeded to make the necessary inquiries respecting the Ground which remained vacant or undisposed of on the scite *[sic]* of Carlton Palace and the adjacent Buildings.

That the result of the information obtained by them was such as to induce the Committee to come to an opinion, that no eligible space of Ground could thus be obtained with reference to the convenience and wants of such a Body as the United University Club.[*28]

Frustrated in that direction, for the next eighty years never a decade passed without some attempt to find an alternative. In 1835 the club architect, Gandy-Deering, was asked to look for other sites – possibly in Pall Mall between the Travellers' and the old Carlton Clubs, or else by purchasing the house just to the east of the existing club house. Like the possibility which had already been discussed in the previous year for an amalgamation with the Oxford and Cambridge in their new house in Pall Mall, which Smirke had vetoed for lack of space, the idea came to nothing.

In 1848 the committee returned to the problem and ordered plans to be drawn up for expansion upwards into an additional storey, but sadly abandoned the idea as impracticable and because of objections from neighbouring tenants. Unable to expand eastwards or upwards, the only possibility left was to purchase the adjoining building – an oil shop – in Suffolk Street itself; but this proved too expensive. Instead, they settled for a general refurbishment of the existing clubhouse: the coffee room, drawing rooms and libraries were redecorated; the house dining room was made into a second coffee room; the ventilation was improved and the cess pools under the building were removed and the club was connected to the sewage system. The Secretary's quarters (two rooms) were converted into bathrooms.[†]

At least the pressure was somewhat eased when in 1853 the committee was able to report to the Annual General Meeting that an extra storey had now been added, providing space for an

---

[*] Carlton House or Palace was demolished in 1826. Waterloo Place had been its forecourt. The committee had evidently been pipped to the post by the United Service Club and the Athenaeum, which the Crown Commissioners had just given permission to build on the corners flanking Pall Mall.

[†] Bathrooms, not considered necessary in the 1820s, were now coming into vogue: 'They never gave me a bath when I was a boy. First house of my own, I had one put in – people used to come and stare at it – in 1840'. – James Forsyte in John Gals – worthy. *A Modern Comedy* (Penguin ed. 1982, vol. 3, p. 646).

additional billiard room, five new dressing rooms, a new office and bedroom for the Secretary and ten new bedrooms for the servants.*

The problem had been ameliorated but not really solved. Spasmodically throughout the 1860s attempts were made to purchase adjoining property, but they were not proceeded with 'owing to the exorbitant demands of the present occupiers'.[29] At last in 1872 the club was able to take a lease on No. 24 Suffolk Street, immediately opposite on the west side, which provided extra space for servants and for a committee room, thereby releasing space in the main club house for another smoking room and billiard room.† At the Annual General Meeting there was much outspoken opposition to the whole idea, since in order to pay for it all it was necessary to raise the subscription from six guineas to seven: however, the motion to do so was finally carried by 135 votes to 45.

Throughout the 1880s and 1890s various sites for a new club house were considered, including 5 St James's Square, Waterloo House, 18 Carlton House Terrace, the Watercolour Society next door to the club – even sites as far afield as Piccadilly and 34 Dover Street: all were turned down for various reasons. Nos 48–51 Pall Mall (opposite the Oxford and Cambridge Club) was another possibility, along with part of the old War Office site where the Royal Automobile Club now stands.

What finally brought matters to a head was the committee's report to the Annual General Meeting in 1904 that the club's financial condition was parlous since expenditure was exceeding income; that the club house not being up to modern standards, the waiting list was declining and many candidates were withdrawing or not taking up their election. In consequence a special committee was set up under the chairmanship of the Lord Chief

---

* But not yet for members. In 1874 the Secretary was still telling enquirers 'There are no bedrooms in the Club for members, but there are several houses in the vicinity where bedrooms can be obtained'. (Secretary's Letter Book, 24 May 1874).
† No. 24 occupied part of the site where Barclay's Bank now stands. It was connected to the main club house by a subway (is it still there?).

Justice, Lord Alverstone. At an Extraordinary General Meeting in May they reported that unless the club was prepared to take a lease on the whole block they would have to leave Suffolk Street. The special committee reported twice more at General Meetings in 1905: they had looked at various sites in Pall Mall, King Street St James's and St James's Square, but they were all too expensive. A site in Cleveland Row had been considered, but King Edward had decided he did not want a club house so close to St James's Palace. At last, the Commissioners for Woods and Forests relented and granted the club a new lease on the Suffolk Street site at a ground rent of £750 *per annum* for the first nine years – a decision greeted by the General Meeting with cheers. It was a modest enough increase; the original ground rent had been £400. The club thereupon went into suspended animation for eighteen months while the house was rebuilt. The members were offered hospitality by the three other university clubs. The staff of fifty-five was cut to twenty-one, seven at each of the clubs offering hospitality. The two General Meetings held in 1906 to discuss future arrangements were held at the Metropole Hotel.

When P. C. Hardwick, the club architect since 1852, retired in 1878, the committee had appointed A. W. (later Sir Arthur) Blomfield. However, he had died in 1899, so it was his nephew, R. A. (later Sir Reginald) Blomfield who was commissioned to rebuild the club, for which he produced a Baroque design with a French flavour – just the sort of thing to appeal to the Edwardian taste for opulence. * Though confined to a site of the same dimensions as Wilkins's club house (106 ft by 53 ft), the new one, by virtue of its extra height, contrived to be much roomier. Externally rather a sore thumb alongside the restrained Regency elegance of the rest of Nash's Suffolk Street, Blomfield nevertheless managed to retain internally the private-house scale of the original – all in marked contrast to the palatial rooms at the Oxford

---

* Though Blomfield was already fifty, most of his better-known work such as the Quadrant, Regent Street and the Menin Gate War Memorial at Ypres dates from the inter-war years. Pevsner is dismissive about his Suffolk Street club house – 'one of Sir Reginald Blomfield's essays in the Champs-Elysées style'. (N. Pevsner. *The Buildings of England: London*, p. 575).

Sir Reginald Blomfield by Ginsbury, c. 1906

The UUC as rebuilt by Sir Reginald Blomfield

and Cambridge. The coffee room, which in the old club house had been on the ground floor looking on to Pall Mall East, was moved to the first floor and the ground floor rooms became smoking rooms. The club had decided to retain the lease on No. 24, using the upper floors as staff quarters, so there was now room on the upper floors of the club house for ten bedrooms for members – an innovation which turned out to be a great success, bringing the club a steady profit of about £200 a year. To help pay for all this, subscriptions were raised by a guinea (from eight guineas to nine): fortunately, there were no Haringtons in Suffolk Street. To meet the immediate cost the club borrowed £25,000 from an insurance company at £3-17-6%. It was hoped at the 1906 Annual General Meeting that the club house would be ready by April 1907: it was, and in fact members were able to hold their next AGM there in May.

At the same time as Suffolk Street was being rebuilt, the committee at the Oxford and Cambridge Club were contemplating changes and in June 1906 they commissioned the architect –

Blomfield again – to prepare sketch plans for various alterations and additions which they thought to be desirable. These included an elaborate enlargement of the strangers' dining room, major alterations to the main staircase, which included lining the walls with much marble and incorporating a large Doric Venetian window to light it, and building an extra storey to provide space for ten bedrooms for members.* Blomfield's plans were ready by October but the committee, no doubt still smarting from the mauling they had received from members over the Harington affair, prudently decided to do nothing till they had put the proposals to the next Annual General Meeting in May 1907. Accordingly these proposals were circulated to all members in April. Objections were not long in coming: one member (Mr E. H. Cardwell) circulated a printed counterblast to the committee's proposals. First, he argued, there was the expense (the estimates were bound to be too low): second, the addition of bedrooms would entirely alter the character of the club, and there was no demand for them anyway: third, with only twenty-six years of the lease left to run, it was an extravagance: and finally the long period (six months) for which the club would have to close would be a great inconvenience.

The committee protested that Mr Cardwell had got his facts wrong, but at the AGM the bedrooms proposal was defeated by a majority of four (87 votes to 83). The other alterations went ahead, however, and the club closed from August to 1 November so that they could be carried out, members being accommodated at the Devonshire Club and the newly-completed United University. The opportunity was taken to redecorate all the principal rooms.

When the club house re-opened, the *Daily Telegraph's* reporter at any rate was ecstatic.

Yesterday was opened again to its members an old Club in Pall-mall which has been entirely renovated in such excellent taste that it will

---

* Enlarging the strangers' dining room involved the demolition of a weight-bearing wall: hence the hefty columns put in to take its place, which seem too large for the room (now the wine bar). The rather bilious Skyros marble round the staircase was no doubt a concession to the Edwardian love of opulence: all right in a bank, perhaps.

now take its right place among the most beautiful houses in London. The Oxford and Cambridge Club House was designed by Smirke, and built on crown property in 1837, and the wonderfully successful transformation of the interior just effected by the skill of Mr Reginald Blomfield, ARA, and an industrious sub-committee affords the first real instance of the latest modern methods being artistically and efficiently combined with the dignity of the old-fashioned style of building. Architecturally, the original design was one of the best that Smirke ever produced; but the Pompeian decorations on a ground of coffee and stone colour, for which Crace was responsible in 1868, never did justice to the noble lines of the structure, and produced a heavy and stuffy effect under which succeeding generations of University members have suffered more or less silently.

It is not often that the committee of a club are either able to carry out reforms of so extremely costly a nature as these must have been, or fortunate enough to find an architect as capable as Mr Blomfield in combining the newest exigencies of modern luxury with the spacious but occasionally over-Spartan architectural plans of seventy years ago.[30]

Mr Cardwell was wrong about the bedrooms. It will be recalled that in 1911 the committee had become concerned about the shrinkage of the waiting lists and had set up a special sub-committee to find out what was wrong. Its diagnosis was as follows:

... The waiting list has seriously deteriorated since 1907 – it was then 666 and is now [1912] 578 – and a great difficulty is found in obtaining candidates who are prepared to take up election. No less than 200 were written to to secure 46 for the last election. This state of affairs in the opinion of the Sub-Committee is largely due to the fact that the two other University Clubs are provided with bedroom accommodation, which has proved to be highly remunerative.[31]

They recommended going ahead with Blomfield's 1907 scheme for the bedrooms, and this time at the Annual General Meeting the motion to do so was carried. The work was completed that summer.

Thus, as the Edwardian age was about to give way to the Georgian, it seemed that the university clubs had faced up to and had overcome their problems. Their club houses were in good order (at the New University they had even managed to acquire the freehold), their membership lists were full. Club servants were still plentiful (59 at the New, 62 at the United University and 68 at the Oxford and Cambridge) as well as cheap: wages were more or less the same as they had been in 1860 – in 1914 the total annual wages bill at the Oxford and Cambridge, excluding the secretary, was £3,000. The average price in the coffee room for lunch was 1/5: in the evening a six-course dinner of soup, fish, entrée, joint, sweet and savoury could be had for 4/- (3d extra if poultry or games were served). The company – with just a few exceptions – was congenial and the future looked secure. It may not have been paradise, but it was a pretty good earthly imitation.

Notes to Chapter II

1. Edward Gibbon. *Decline and Fall of the Roman Empire*, ch. III
2. John Buchan. *Memory Hold-The-Door*, pp. 92–4
3. UUC AGMM 1833, 1846, 1861; GCM, 3 January 1878 and 1 January 1885
4. J. Britton. 'The University Club House, Suffolk Street' in J. Britton and A. Pugin. *Public Buildings of London*, vol. II, p. 253
5. OC GCM, 20 April 1883
6. OC GCM, 16 January 1891. The UUC anecdote is recorded in Charles Graves, *Leather Armchairs*
7. T. H. S. Escott. *Club Makers and Club Members*, p. 245
8. UUC GCM, 6 June 1832
9. UUC GCM, 18 December 1862; NUC GCM, 18 November 1873
10. OC GCM, 2 March 1900
11. UUC GCM, 31 May 1838
12. J. M. Scott. *The Book of Pall Mall*, p. 126, quoting the report in *The Morning Post*
13. OC GCM, 25 November 1887
14. UUC GCM, 17 November 1897
15. UUC AGMM, 25 May 1932
16. Charles Crawley. *Trinity Hall*, pp. 152–6
17. Graves. *op. cit.*
18. Arthur Griffiths, *Clubs and Clubmen*, p. 199
19. UUC GCM, 17 May 1888
20. UUC AGMM 1870
21. UUC EGMM 1871
22. UUC EGMM, 22 June 1874
23. OC GCM, 17 November 1865
24. OC GCM, 16 January 1903
25. Law Reports *Harington v. Sendall* reported in [1903] 1, Ch. 921
26. OC AGM, 18 May 1904
27. UUC AGM 1829
28. UUC AGM 1829
29. UUC AGM 1870
30. *Daily Telegraph*, 2 November 1907
31. OC GCM, 26 March 1912

Chapter III

Fortunes of War

For the first seven months of 1914 the committee at the Oxford and Cambridge had only to concern itself with the humdrum routine of running a club. They signed the cheques (three signatures on each) to Bellamy's (for poultry), to Paxton's (for butter and ham), to Jackson's (for groceries), to Lambert & Butler (for cigars), to Fortnum & Mason's (for cigarettes). They made arrangements at Lord's for the Oxford and Cambridge and the Eton and Harrow matches (nine arbours to be taken for each, with luncheon tickets at eight shillings). They approached the Commissioners for Woods and Forests for an extension of the lease. They dealt with a complaint from a member that another member's guest had been smoking in the morning room.

The coming of war in August presented them with new and less familiar problems. Two reservists among the club servants at Suffolk Street were recalled to the colours and five others volunteered: their jobs were to be kept open for them and their wages paid in full. Future volunteers were promised that they would not be losers pecuniarily. At the New University Club the Secretary, Captain Rowe, went off to war almost immediately and had to be replaced by a series of amateur stand-ins. * At Suffolk Street

---

* This was to have quite serious consequences for the club. Perhaps unavoidably, more and more authority devolved to the Steward. It only came to light in 1920 that he and the Chef had been systematically robbing the club by taking and selling food. However, in view of the Steward's past services to the club he was exonerated, largely on the character evidence of Captain Rowe.

a member suggested 'That unmarried club waiters be offered liberal terms if they enlist for the war ... and that if they do not avail themselves of the chance, their services be dispensed with'.[1] This of course was only the start of what was to become a major manpower problem: at the 1915 AGM the committee reported that the club was having to employ female staff as men and boys were unobtainable: by March 1916 the Oxford and Cambridge committee had to empower the secretary to engage girls instead of page boys: in May he had to inform the committee that the chef and his two assistants were leaving to join the army, and by June 1917 waitresses had replaced waiters in the coffee room.

As early as October 1914 both of these clubs decided to insure their houses 'against all damage, directly or indirectly caused from Aerial Craft, including Bombs or Missiles issuing there-from',[2] a prescient step, for at this early stage few could have foreseen the bombing of London which did in fact occur, first by Zeppelins and later by Gotha bombers. As it turned out, the only damage sustained was to the roof of the Oxford and Cambridge Club in February 1918, caused by the cap of one of our own anti-aircraft shells – a contingency presumably not covered by the terms of the policy. Still, the air raids were real enough: in all, 1,414 were killed and 3,146 were injured in Britain by bombing raids in this war – proportionately very heavy casualties for the tonnage of bombs actually dropped. * With almost sublime ego-tism one member complained that he could not get the smoking room bell answered during the air raid on 30 September 1917 (the committee in reply approved the Steward's action in directing the staff to take cover during the raid): another complained that because of it part of his dinner was not served, and could he therefore please have two shillings refunded (the request was granted).

At all three clubs hospitality was extended to various categories of serving officers who found themselves working in London and were duly qualified, such as those in the Anti-Aircraft Corps, officers of the colonial forces, and (at Suffolk

---

* The clubs took whatever precautions they could: hence an item in the Oxford and Cambridge Club accounts for November 1917: 'Sandbags for windows £5.0.0'.

Street) officers on active service or who had held field rank before retirement and who had no London club (though by the 1915 AGM it appears that only five had availed themselves of the privilege). Later, all three clubs agreed to take in as temporary honorary members American officers who were members of the University Clubs of New York, Philadelphia or Boston.

When the Germans reverted to unrestricted submarine warfare in January 1917 and allied shipping losses mounted frighteningly, food and other shortages really began to bite. In September the historian F. S. Oliver wrote to his brother in Canada:

It sometimes occurs to me to wonder if you, at the other side of an ocean and a continent, can form an adequate picture of the lives of your friends and relations over here: of a London whose wheeled traffic, I suppose, must have been reduced by about two-thirds; whose nights are dark and sometimes almost as silent as the country; where nearly all the necessaries of life, except air and water, have to be bought in the most sparing quantities, and have to be paid for on the average at something more than twice the old prices; where at any public place you are allowed no more than two tiny lumps of sugar (together not much more than half the size of the old-fashioned lump); where coal, coke, matches and everything of that nature have to be husbanded as if they were heaps of gold.

Of course, the result of this is not by any means all bad. I never knew till last summer what a delicious thing a potato was, that is, when I couldn't buy any; nor did I ever realise the transcendent luxury of white bread.[3]

Naturally, these rigours affected the clubs to some extent. Earlier in the war some economies had been made, though there was an air of tokenism about them: at Suffolk Street, for example, the committee resolved in June 1915 that no veal or lamb should be served till further notice – presumably on the grounds that fully-grown cattle and sheep would feed more people. Later in the same year at the Oxford and Cambridge the portions of meat were reduced and cigars were rationed (no member to be allowed to buy more than one hundred at a time nor more than five hundred in a year). When shortages became real, in 1917, all the clubs decided to introduce one meatless day per week (Friday) and two potatoless days (Monday and Thursday), but quickly rescinded their decision pending clarification by the War Cabinet (the objection was people would only eat more breadstuffs, and they were in even shorter supply). Later in the year, however, potatoes and cream disappeared from the menu altogether: sugar was no longer served in the coffee room and members, at the request of the Board of Trade, were encouraged to use spills so as to economise on matches. At Suffolk Street in 1918 the strangers' dining room was closed for lunches: members could feed their guests in the coffee room, but only one per day. At the Oxford and Cambridge a half-coupon was required for two ounces of cooked meat and butter was only supplied at breakfast.

In April 1915 the Reverend Fox Lambert (a member in Pall Mall) had written to the committee asking whether it would be expedient and possible to persuade members 'to follow the lead of the King and Lord Kitchener with regard to Alcoholic Liquors'.[4] The committee, realising that there must be limits to patriotism and knowing their members better than Fox Lambert did, replied firmly that it would not. Nevertheless, the comparison between consumption in 1913 and 1918 reveals some interesting variations.[*] Spirits seem to have presented no problem, for in March 1916 the wine committee was still able to obtain two hogsheads of Scotch whisky, albeit at two shillings more a gallon than they had paid in the past.

Food and staff shortages, however, were temporary problems, which would disappear when war ended. What were more worrying were the two problems which would dog the clubs off and on for the next fifty years – namely, rising costs unmatched by equivalent rises in income. In 1919 the committee of the

[*]	1913	1918
Claret	159 dozen	96 dozen
Burgundy	41 ,,	50 ,,
Chablis, Graves, Sauternes	20 ,,	78 ,,
Hock & Moselle	101 ,,	9 ,,
Sherry & Madeira	62 ,,	70 ,,

No figures were given for champagne or port. There seems to have been no grave shortage of the latter, though, since in 1918 the Wine Committee decided to sell off some of the '63.

Oxford and Cambridge Club estimated that since 1914 costs had doubled, an estimate exactly borne out by the official retail price index. Staff wages rose too, though not as fast as other costs: by 1919 the wage bill, £3,000 in 1914, had only risen to about £3,500. In November the club's auditors recommended an increase in subscriptions from nine guineas to twelve. Though this led to a few resignations, the proposed increase was carried unanimously at an Extraordinary General Meeting held in the following month.

At the 1916 AGM at the United University Club the committee reported that the club was running at a deficit, mainly due to the war, and that it would be necessary to appeal to members to make a voluntary contribution (any increase in subscription, they felt, would be difficult in view of the Harington Judgment). At the 1917 AGM they reported that just over half the membership had responded to the appeal, in sums ranging from one pound to a hundred, and that this had so far produced a total of £3,138.3s.

But an appeal of this kind could only be a temporary expedient: the real problem went deeper, as the Chairman explained to an Extraordinary General Meeting called later in the year. The normal pre-war membership of the club had been about a thousand (in 1914 it was 1,022): it was now down to 860, so income was down by £1,500 a year. And whereas before the war the club normally elected about forty new members annually, only twenty-seven had come forward in the past year. The loss in entrance fees was therefore about six to seven hundred pounds. Estimated net losses for the current year were £1,500 to £2,000 (matters were not helped by the fact that over a tenth of the members were serving at the front and in consequence were on the absentee list and were paying only two guineas instead of the full subscription). The committee's proposal was that the club should admit a hundred new members without entrance fee, each paying eleven guineas instead of nine, thereby producing an additional £1,100 a year. So as not to block normal elections later, it was proposed that such members should be aged over thirty. The scheme seemed an ingenious one: by only charging new members the higher rate it got round the problem of the Harington Judgment and by waiving the entrance fee it eliminated the chief obstacle to recruiting new members. But the committee failed to persuade the Meeting and the proposal was lost.

Much the same problem was being encountered at the New University Club: there, in 1914, they had sought to boost membership by introducing a 'nominated candidate' scheme, whereby each member could, once and only once, nominate a candidate for admission without entrance fee.

In point of fact all three clubs were extremely worried about where future members were going to come from. In view of the war they had all dropped the residence qualification from their rules, but that did not solve the problem, which was that for four years the universities had been virtually denuded of undergraduates. Without the seed-corn whence would come the harvest? Aware of this, the Chairman of the Oxford and Cambridge Club reported in November 1915 to the committee that he had had a discussion with the Chairman of the UUC about the possibility of amalgamation (possibly as the United Oxford and Cambridge University Club) in Suffolk Street, where they were planning to extend the premises. The committee agreed that such talk was probably premature; but a year later they were concerned to hear rumours of a possible merger between the UUC and the NUC, and asked that a joint committee should be set up to consider the future of all the united clubs. In December 1916 a joint meeting was held: the Oxford and Cambridge representative said he was apprehensive that the supply of future candidates might not be sufficient to sustain three university clubs. The Chairman of the NUC (Sir Charles Lucas), however, said that he did not share this view and intended to carry on. He also denied the rumour of a merger with the UUC. So there the matter rested for the next twenty years.

Unlike the Public Schools Club which was simply wiped out by the war and had to be re-founded afterwards, the university clubs escaped comparatively lightly. The one we know most about, since at the 1919 AGM the members voted unanimously to compile a Roll of Honour not just of those who had been killed in action but of all those who had served in the forces, is the New University Club. Though essentially a non-military club, 349 of its 1,100 members, many of whom were over military age, served with the armed forces.* Of the 225 who served overseas either on the Western Front or in the so-called sideshows in Gallipoli or Salonika or Mesopotamia, forty-five were killed and seventy-five were wounded, many more than once.† Between them they earned eighteen DSOs, forty-three MCs, twenty-three OBEs, twenty-three foreign decorations and ninety-two mentions in dispatches.

At Suffolk Street the first report of the death of a member in action came in March 1915: it was Second Lieutenant W. G. Fletcher, Royal Welch Fusiliers, who was killed at Neuve Chapelle. By May 1916, shortly before the Battle of the Somme, there were 122 members serving. By the end of the war forty members had died. As was the way, nearly all of these were captains and subalterns. It must not be assumed, however, that they were all striplings, just down from university: the photographs in the United University Club's Roll of Honour are often of mature men, including one grey-haired Second Lieutenant in the Black Watch.

By April 1916, 167 members and twenty-one staff of the Oxford and Cambridge Club were in the armed services: by the end, thirty-five had died.

> *The world's great age begins anew,*
> *The golden years return ...*

– or so Lord Curzon, quoting Shelley, assured the House of Lords when war ended in 1918. But it was not going to be quite like that, at any rate for the clubs. True, the return to normality

---

* As early as November 1914 80% of the members of the Public Schools Club were on active service and by the end of the war 800 had been killed in action. The Sports Club – another young members' club – lost 216 members and staff. The service clubs, naturally, also suffered badly.
† In addition to these, of the sixteen club servants who joined up, two were killed and six were wounded.

came much more quickly than it would at the end of the Second World War. Food rationing, for example, which had only started in December 1917 with sugar, began to be dismantled in July 1918 and was gone by November 1920, whereas after the second war butter and meat rationing lingered on till 1954. The labour unrest of the early 1920s caused some inconvenience and apprehension: the coal shortage in 1919 had led the Oxford and Cambridge's committee to suggest that one of the three clubs should close each month (it did not happen) and in 1920 the UUC made enquiries about insuring against burglary consequent on civil riots. In April 1921 the miners' strike very quickly led to a 50% cut in coal allowance to the clubs: the consequent economies meant (in Pall Mall) a reduction in the number of hot dishes at lunch from four to three, and (in Arlington Street) 'in view of the coal strike the committee decided that no hot baths were to be provided in the morning'.[5]

But these were trivia and soon forgotten. What was much more serious and would not go away was the fact that costs were still rising and clubs were running at a deficit. At the AGM in 1919 the Chairman of the UUC reported that there had recently been a meeting of chairmen of eighteen West End clubs who had all agreed that, the Harington Judgment notwithstanding, they would have to raise subscriptions to at least twelve guineas. At the Oxford and Cambridge the club's auditors likewise recommended an increase from nine guineas to twelve, and in fact at an Extraordinary General Meeting in December a resolution to do so was carried unanimously: it provoked some resignations and, not for the first nor the last time, a few proposals for a concession for country members. At Arlington Street the committee sent a circular to all members proposing an increase to thirteen guineas from nine, though with concessionary rates of six guineas and three guineas respectively to undergraduate and supernumerary members (those absent abroad). The increases in costs since 1914 were, it explained:

Rates and taxes	150%	Gas and electricity	60%
Wages	50%	Servants' Liveries	170%

| Board wages | 100% | Laundry | 80% |
| Coal | 180% | Newspapers, etc. | 120%[6]. |

The club lost a hundred members in consequence, but the EGM in November agreed to the increase. To later generations inured to inflation, such things may seem nothing out of the normal: to a generation brought up in pre-war stability, when a sovereign had been a sovereign, and moreover to one whose incomes had probably increased little and were now much more heavily taxed, the phenomenon was a painful and alarming one.*

There was at any rate one respect in which their worst fears turned out to be groundless: the labour unrest which had induced the committee at Suffolk Street to investigate insurance against riot and civil commotion soon subsided. The General Strike in 1926, which had induced in some alarmists apocalyptic visions of the gutters of St James's running blue with blood, proved a nine days' wonder: the only ripple in any of the clubs' records is an Oxford and Cambridge committee resolution:

Arising out of the General Strike at midnight on the 3rd May, it was decided to remit the bedroom rental charge in cases where it was known that a member was unable to occupy the room by reason of the failure of transport facilities.[7]

Hardly the stuff of revolution.

When the United University Club rebuilt their club house in 1907 they had decided to hang on to No. 24 on the other side of the street, since it provided a useful overflow for offices and staff quarters. However, Barclay's Bank had their eye on this site for a new branch, and in 1914 they had offered the club the leases of Nos 20 and 21 in exchange for the surrender of the lease on No. 24. The committee were not too interested in 20 and 21 but had long been keen to acquire Nos 2, 3 and 4 which were next door to the club house itself. Eventually, after some complicated legal wheeling and dealing the details of which are lost in the mists of time, they agreed to exchange the club's interest in the lease of

---

* Standard rate of income tax in 1914 had been 1/2d in the pound: by 1920 it was 6/-, though it fell to 4/- by 1926. In 1914 surtax began at £3,000, but by 1920 it began at £2,000.

No. 24 to Barclay's Bank in exchange for the interest now held in Nos 2, 3 and 4 by a third party (Messrs Steadman van Praagh). These would provide extra space for another smoking room and a card room and for some more bedrooms for both members and staff. The intention was to rebuild these houses when the war was over and the labour market had settled down and the existing sub-tenants (Humphrey and Crooke, the army tailors, and Stoddart and Co., wine merchants) could be got rid of. In 1920 the club architect – still Blomfield – was commissioned and in the following year the Commissioners for Woods and Forests, the ground landlords, gave the go-ahead. Work began in May 1923, the club house remaining partly open throughout the work: it was completed in the following year. Now at last the club had the extra space it needed and had badly lacked for a century.

Four years of wartime neglect meant that the Oxford and Cambridge Club too was in need of refurbishment and repair. In July 1919 the committee sent a circular to all members asking them to subscribe to the cost, which they estimated would come to £9,435, with another £1,500 to instal central heating.* Apparently the money was forthcoming, for in July 1920 the club closed for three months for the work to be carried out: as was customary in such eventualities, the other university clubs provided hospitality, as did the Sports and East India Clubs and the now defunct United Service and British Empire Clubs. As well as redecoration some minor alterations were made in the staff mess room and recreation room. When the club re-opened *The Field* commented:

So many of our readers are members of the Oxford and Cambridge Club that they will be glad to hear of its reopening on October 18 after being closed for thirteen weeks ... The spacious and well-proportioned apartments look twice as well as they ever did.

Old customs die hard, and rightly so; but the Oxford and Cambridge Club is rapidly achieving a blend of the best of the old with the soundest of the new that almost rivals its still admirable cellar.[8]

---

* Heating of the main rooms was of course by coal fires, though at some stage these had been replaced by anthracite stoves. In December 1921 the committee decided to revert to coal fires, and the anthracite stoves were sold off to members.

The bedrooms which Blomfield had added just before the war had proved so popular and such a useful source of extra income that the hunt was on for more. When the Guards' Club next door at 69 and 70 Pall Mall was demolished in 1919, the site was acquired by the London, Joint City and Midland Bank. The committee hoped that it might be possible to acquire the upper floors of the new building for extra bedrooms for the club. Negotiations dragged on until the middle of 1922, but eventually were abandoned because of the cost. Instead, the club decided to acquire a hostel for staff at 27 St George's Road in Pimlico, thereby releasing a staff dormitory at the top of the club house for conversion to members' bedrooms. That proposal was accepted (this time without cavilling from the more conservative members): the staff hostel was acquired on a twelve-year lease for £1,700 and provided accommodation for sixteen men and eight boys. It was still going strong in 1950.

During these inter-war years it fell to both of the older clubs to celebrate their centenaries with a dinner, which they duly did, the UUC in 1922 and the Oxford and Cambridge in 1930 (they celebrated again in 1938 to mark the centenary of the opening of the club house). When Stanley Baldwin, who had been a member at Suffolk Street since 1893, became Chancellor of Cambridge, the club arranged a dinner in January 1932 to mark the event. Sir Austen Chamberlain, a member since 1902, took the chair and the Prince of Wales attended, together with 212 other members – which must have made for a great squash in the Suffolk Street coffee room.* There were other events to celebrate, too, as the 1930s passed: both clubs erected stands for George V's silver jubilee procession and were soon planning again to do likewise for Edward VIII's coronation: in Pall Mall tickets costing eight guineas, to include breakfast and a champagne lunch, were balloted for. Prudently as it turned out the committee also took out £2,000-worth of insurance in case the coronation did not take place When George VI's finally did in 1937 the club marked the event by giving the entire staff an extra four days' pay.

* The full text of both Baldwin's and Austen Chamberlain's speeches are preserved in the club archives. Both are masterly examples of the art of saying nothing elegantly.

CENTENARY DINNER

OF THE

OXFORD AND CAMBRIDGE UNIVERSITY CLUB.

❧

WEDNESDAY, 21ST MAY, 1930.

Though the constituent elements of the clubs' memberships had changed but little over the first century of their existence, the proportions had. The clergy, for example, who had been so predominant in Victorian and Edwardian times, were by the interwar years greatly reduced. At Suffolk Street in the 1830s they had constituted between a quarter and a third of the total membership. Their numbers were now down to fifty-eight – less than one-twentieth, of whom perhaps the best known was Dean Inge of St Paul's.* At the Oxford and Cambridge Club there had originally been 190: now there were less than half that number. Despite the fact that both clubs could field a past or future Prime Minister and a past Foreign Secretary (Baldwin and Austen Chamberlain in Suffolk Street, Attlee and Sir Edward Grey in Pall Mall) both together contained only a dozen Members of Parliament.

The bench and the bar, on the other hand, were if anything more strongly represented than ever: Rayner Goddard, a future Lord Chief Justice, was a member of the UUC,† as was Lord Sterndale, Master of the Rolls, 1919–23. His successor in that office, Lord Hanworth, was a member of the Oxford and Cambridge. Two Lord Chancellors – Lord Sankey, in Ramsay Macdonald's ministry, and Lord Dilhorne (Sir Reginald Manningham-Buller) in Harold Macmillan's second ministry – were members there too. At all three clubs the academic connection remained strong. Dr Adrian of Trinity (subsequently Lord Adrian, Master of the College), who won the Nobel Prize for Medicine and Physiology in 1932, was the NUC's Cambridge resident representative in the 1920s and 1930s: he was succeeded in that role by the historian, G. S. R. Kitson Clark, in 1937. Another historian, R. C. K. Ensor, who contributed the 1870–1914 volume to the *Oxford History of England*, was a member of the UUC: so was (Sir) Henry Tizard, the scientist to whom so much is owed for his work on the Radar/VHF air

* 'The Gloomy Dean', a considerable publicist in the 1930s; as one critic put it, 'from being a pillar of the Church, he became a column in the *Standard*'.
† Perhaps it was his reputation as a hanging judge which led the committee of the club to invite him to chair any AGM where trouble was particularly expected.

defence system in the 1930s: he became Rector of Imperial College.* E. H. Carr, historian of the Russian Revolution, was a member of the Oxford and Cambridge in this period, as was Arnold Toynbee.

A section of the membership of increasing importance in these years was that involved in home and imperial administration, frequently at a very senior level. (Sir) Edward Bridges, son of the Poet Laureate, was a member at Suffolk Street: he was Secretary to the Cabinet from 1938 to 1947 and Head of the Civil Service from 1945 to 1946. He went on to become Chancellor of Reading University. Lord Chelmsford, another member, was Viceroy of India from 1916 to 1921. Charles Bathurst (Viscount Bledisloe), a member of the Oxford and Cambridge Club, was Governor-General of New Zealand in the 1930s.

It is a comfort to find that the same club was at last able to provide us with a more than minor literary figure in the person of T. S. Eliot. The library is in consequence the fortunate possessor of inscribed copies of most of his plays and the collected poems. In quite another direction the membership included a distinguished athlete in the person of Maxwell Woosnam, a quadruple Cambridge blue (for football, golf, lawn and real tennis) who went on to become a double international (for soccer and lawn tennis). If nothing else, it was a pretty all-round sort of club.

A less distinguished but nevertheless prominent and popular club figure at Suffolk Street in these years (and indeed up to his death shortly before the amalgamation) was Major R. H. Sampson. Born in 1896 and educated at Rugby, he won an exhibition in mathematics to Cambridge but was prevented from going up by the First World War. Between the wars he was a chartered accountant. A very regular attender at the club and involved on many of its committees and sub-committees (especially the wine committee) – he even served as acting secretary on several occasions when the secretary was absent – he had a sideline as a successful writer of murder stories, several of which were

---

* He also found time to serve on the committee and several sub-committees of the club.

reprinted in the Penguin crime library. One of these is clearly set in the United University Club, thinly disguised as 'The Whitehall Club'. *

In November 1932 when the United University Club advertised the post of Steward in the *Daily Telegraph* at a wage of four pounds a week, it received 450 applications. Earlier in the year the Chairman had told the Annual General Meeting that the membership was twenty-four short of capacity and the waiting list had been completely wiped out. By 1936 it was thirty-two short; by 1937 seventy-two. These were of course two symptoms of one phenomenon – the depression and unemployment following (though not directly consequent upon) the Wall Street Crash of 1929. Many clubs were hit hard – some, such as the Cavendish and the New Oxford and Cambridge, were extinguished by it. The life style adopted in most London clubs might be described as that appropriate to what Arnold Bennett once called the 'solid middle class'. The problem was that not all club members commanded the income necessary to sustain a solid middle-class life style: they merely aspired to it. The university clubs, where a significant proportion of the members were young, were particularly hit when times were depressed. The one most deeply affected was the New University Club.

Matters had been rather unsettled there ever since the war had ended. Just as they had been at Suffolk Street before Blomfield had re-built the club house, members at St James's Street were growing discontented with the club house which Waterhouse had built for them in the 1860s. When, therefore, the club received an offer in October 1919 of £120,000 for their freehold, the committee took it seriously and started looking elsewhere for an alternative. One was quickly found at 20 St James's Square,

---

* *Keep it Quiet.* Faber 1935, republished by Penguin in 1954. The author wrote under the pseudonym of Richard Hull. An unedifying tale in which two members are poisoned, the secretary is terrorised and a county court judge steals the library books. The murderer (another member) very properly commits suicide so that, rather than bring the club into disrepute, the whole affair can be hushed up. Most erudite on the question of choosing his poisons, it seems more than likely that Major Sampson had consulted another member of the UUC, Sir Bernard Spilsbury, the Home Office Pathologist.

and the committee sought a refusal at £60,000. However, none was available, they were told, since two other offers existed. They nevertheless decided to favour the sale of their existing house for £140,000 plus, provided they could get 20 St James's Square for under £70,000.* At an Extraordinary General Meeting called for 21 October the Chairman, Lieutenant-Colonel J. H. M. Greenly, outlined to members the snags of the present house:

Its rooms though fine are unnecessarily high and appear cold and comfortless when judged by the standards of today: it has an unnecessarily large amount of waste space that cannot be utilized and yet that must be kept clean and decorated: the bedroom accommodation is extremely limited: its service arrangements are in many respects awkward and even insanitary: its lavatory accommodation could well be improved on ... It is difficult to heat adequately without a very large expenditure of fuel: it has no accommodation for ladies should such be considered desirable: and lastly its architecture cannot be described as one of its attractions.

Truly tastes had changed since the Victorian enthusiasm for Gothic romanticism. He went on to describe the advantages of St James's Square: it was bigger (8,460 square feet as against the present club's 7,000 square feet) and there were twenty bedrooms and room for ladies. It even had a laundry. Moreover,

It is a very striking example of an Adam house, almost unique in its perfection. It is exceedingly well situated in the centre of Clubland, on the west side of St James's Square, two doors south of King Street.[9]

How could the members possibly resist such sales-talk? The motion to sell was carried, 137 to 58. Five months later, however, the Chairman had to report that when their present club house had been put up for auction on 15 March 1920 there had been no genuine bids nor any subsequent offers. By the end of May, although several prospective purchasers had shown interest, in the event none could find the money.

---

* When they received the £120,000 offer the committee had sought an independent valuation from the firm of John D. Wood. With the insouciant optimism of all estate agents, John D. Wood valued the existing club house at between £140,000 and £175,000.

Nothing further happened for several years, though from time to time the committee did look at several nearby premises which came on the market in the hope of finding space for more bedrooms. One possibility was the Ladies' Club at 9 Arlington Street, which was moving to larger premises in 1923, but it came to nothing. Eventually in October 1929 the club received an offer of £130,000 from an American syndicate wishing to redevelop the whole site as an hotel. Interest revived and the committee seriously considered taking 20 Arlington Street as a possible alternative site for a club house (the asking price was £90,000); but they regretfully concluded that it was not suitable. One other possibility was No. 4 St James's Square, which was owned by Lord and Lady Astor, but the matter was not pursued. From time to time the club looked at other properties – Spencer House and 4 and 5 Carlton House Terrace among them – but one senses with diminishing conviction, because by the early 1930s the club was feeling more and more acutely the consequences of the depression.

When the committee met in May 1931, 'It was pointed out that this Club, in common with others, was feeling the effect of the present depression and cash was less plentiful':[10] revenue from subscriptions and bedrooms was down £615 on the previous year. Moreover there was a drop in the number of candidates coming forward for election. In 1928 there had been seventy-eight; in 1929 sixty-eight; in 1930 only forty-eight. At an Extraordinary General Meeting in February 1932 called to consider the deteriorating financial position the Chairman had to announce that there had been a hundred resignations.* In a bid to attract more members the meeting decided to abolish the thirty-guineas entrance fee. At the 1934 AGM as a way of boosting income there was a proposal to form a Club Masonic Lodge, but this idea was turned down by referendum. In October 1936 the committee regretfully rejected a proposal to rebuild the club

---

* The Chairman was Lt-Col. Victor Burrow Hill, who survived to become Father of the United Oxford and Cambridge Club. He died in 1986, in his hundredth year, an active user of the club almost till the end. His memory is particularly associated with the annual St Valentine's Day dinner, which he instituted.

house to modern requirements as impracticable, and accepted that there simply was not room for three university clubs in London.

In a final gesture of defiance the 1937 AGM gave the committee authority to try again to draw up a plan to rebuild; but the game was nearly up. In September an offer of £100,000 was received for the freehold, and the sub-committee on finance recommended acceptance. In November the Chairman (Neville Colt) circularised all members recommending selling the club house and listing three options: first, amalgamating with another university club (his own recommendation): second, moving to larger premises to provide more amenities (in his view financially perilous): third, moving to smaller premises with a smaller membership of five to six hundred. At an EGM in the following month which two hundred members attended, a motion to approve the sale and amalgamate with the United University Club was carried (131 in favour, 44 against).

Completion of the sale took place on 20 December. After repayment of debentures the club was left with a balance in cash of £40,000. The club house finally closed on 3 June 1938.

From the UUC's point of view the proposal to amalgamate was a welcome one, for it too had been suffering a decline in membership, though not quite so badly as the other club. By 1932 the full complement of 1,150 was twenty-four short; despite having extended eligibility by requiring only one year's residence instead of two, by 1936 it was thirty-two short and by 1937 seventy-two short. At their March meeting 'the Committee viewed with concern the falling off in Revenue caused by the drop in membership'.[11] At an Extraordinary General Meeting in January 1938 the Chairman explained the terms of the proposed amalgamation: they were, first, that the NUC would bring with them the lump sum of £40,000 already referred to: second, the amalgamated club would have between four and six hundred new members: third, in order to accommodate them all the club would acquire No. 5 Suffolk Street and would extend the club house eastwards to Whitcomb Street. The members present approved the proposal by 144 votes to 76.

To set the final seal, the two clubs held simultaneous EGMs on 27 April 1938, the UUC at the Suffolk Galleries in Suffolk Street, the NUC at the Prince's Restaurant in Piccadilly. The Chairman at Suffolk Street explained the plans for extending the club house in order to provide a 50% increase in coffee room, sitting room and smoking room accommodation. There were to be some extra bedrooms, two squash courts and entirely separate quarters, with its own entrance at the corner of Whitcomb Street, for entertaining ladies at all times of day. At this point in the meeting the news arrived that the NUC had voted in favour of amalgamation (124–28): the United University meeting then voted too and the motion to amalgamate was carried by more than the necessary two-thirds majority (115–32). The effective date was to be 31 May.

This brought the total membership of the club to a healthy 1,496, and at the Annual General meeting in 1939 it was announced that the club house would be closed for the two months of July and August to enable the construction work to go ahead. One member proposed in the Suggestion Book 'that our new cellars be made bomb-proof and gas-proof. We can then preserve our stock of good wines, for the solace of posterity (if any).'

It transpired, however, that Westminster City Council had other uses in mind for the club cellars: when war came in September 1939 the committee received from them a letter stating that the club was under legal obligation to accommodate two hundred members of the general public in the event of an air raid. Perhaps it was this requirement which enabled the club to make use of the breathing-space provided by the six months of phoney war to get permission to go ahead with the building, and work was completed by February 1940, thereby enabling the club to elect two hundred lady associates from the wives, daughters, sisters and mothers of members to occupy the new ladies' wing. At the Oxford and Cambridge Club they had initially decided to close the Ladies' Annex for the duration but, a month into the war, that decision was rescinded.

As in the previous war, both clubs decided to extend

The drawing room of the NUC
Drawing by Sir Muirhead Bone, 1938

temporary membership to up to a hundred 'gentlemen engaged in official war duties in London'.[12] At Suffolk Street they insisted that these should be Oxbridge graduates: at the other end of Pall Mall they were less exclusive. Later, in 1941, when London was full of allied officers in a motley and extraordinary assortment of uniforms from all the allied nations, the UUC granted temporary membership to a limited number of officers of the Belgian, Czech, Dutch and Norwegian armies who were graduates of a foreign university, without payment of a subscription.

To begin with there was no particular hardship to endure other than the blackout which, at any rate for the first few months, was total: not even torches were allowed. Road casualties rose dramatically, but fears of old buffers being set upon by footpads on the very steps of their clubs turned out to be misplaced: there was no marked increase in crimes of violence. When the bombing of London finally began in September 1940 the secretaries very sensibly made arrangements with other clubs to offer each other hospitality should any of them be damaged.

Though neither of the university clubs suffered very serious bomb damage during the war, they did not escape totally: on the night of 26–27 September the Oxford and Cambridge was hit by a couple of incendiary bombs, one of which started a small fire on the roof. It was put out by the staff. Early in October at Suffolk Street the committee recorded their thanks to the Steward and staff for putting out a number of incendiary bombs which landed on and around the club. There were at this time a number of members living more or less permanently in the club: one of them recalls that they

descended the stairs from their bedrooms in the late evening wearing dressing gowns and carrying blankets, pillows and thermos flasks to bed down under the billiard table on the ground floor. The Club's next door neighbour, Hampton's ... received a direct hit in an air raid so their caution was understandable.[13]

On 10 October a bomb exploded outside the Pall Mall smoking room, which closed the club for five or six days: as soon as it re-opened it offered hospitality to the members of the Travellers' and the Reform when they in their turn were damaged. As the club settled to the routine of nightly blitz a regular dormitory for members was set up in the lower billiard room with bunks (use of dormitory 5/- a night, bath 1/- extra): because of the raids, it was decided that dinners should not be served in the coffee room later than 7.30 p.m. At the Oxford and Cambridge Club an air raid shelter had already been arranged in the basement as soon as war began.

Another Suffolk Street member who was living in the club for twelve months during the blitz was John (later Lord) Wolfenden, Headmaster of Uppingham but on secondment to the Air Ministry.

As the year wore on and nightly bombing became routine it was a fairly hot spot, and the morning walk down the Strand to Adastral House provided daily evidence of what had happened the night before. Practically everything round us was hit, hotels, banks, shops, and we never knew, as we got up in the morning, whether there would be water or gas. We developed a blasé indifference, having long ago decided that if we were going to be blown to bits we would rather be warm and comfortable in bed when we were. Only twice did we get up in the middle of the night, when it was just too noisy to sleep. The roster of fire-watching, with other members and with the Club servants, produced a sort of affection for the place which shared discomfort and danger engender.[14]

Apart from the incidents already mentioned there is no record of any further damage to the club house in Suffolk Street. In the case of the Oxford and Cambridge Club it is harder to tell. The minutes for 3 May 1944 note some damage to the bedrooms but not the date or cause. One secondary source records that a land mine penetrated to the kitchen in the basement but failed to explode: however, one must be chary of accepting this, for secondary sources on club history are notoriously unreliable and there is no mention at all of the matter in the club archives which, if indeed it occurred, is remarkable.

There remains the intriguing little mystery of the bullet-like hole in the large mirror which until recently was mounted on the east wall of the smoking room, around which grew over the years

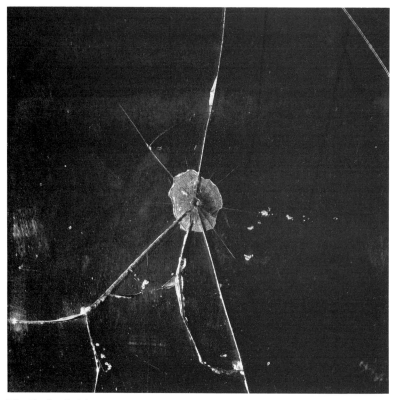

The 'bullet hole'

a small thicket of club mythology: no one seems to be able to speak from first-hand knowledge. The more prosaic and perhaps more likely explanation is that it was caused simply by a piece of flying bomb-splinter or rubble from a bomb which fell in Pall Mall just opposite. A more colourful version which has its adherents is that during the period when invasion seemed likely and all officers in uniform carried side arms, it was customary to leave these on entering the club house with the Hall Porter. While everybody was at lunch a bored page boy took a revolver up to the smoking room and, not realising it was loaded, took aim at his own reflection in the mirror and fired it. If true, and one would like it to be so, he must have given himself the shock of his life.*

* When being taken down in 1990 during refurbishment the mirror was unfortunately smashed. Nevertheless, with due deference to club mythology, the bit with the hole has been carefully framed and is kept in the smoking room.

Largely because the whole question of food supply and rationing was so much better handled by the government in the second war than it had been in the first, food shortages seem to have provided the clubs with fewer problems. By order of the Ministry of Food, clubs, like restaurants, were instructed to restrict lunches and dinners to three courses. At Suffolk Street in December 1942 members were restricted to two guests only at meals (in February 1943 this was further limited to four in a calendar month). Unless members were staying in the clubs for more than a few days, food coupons were not required. There was in any case a wide range of food which, unlike butcher's meat, was unrationed provided it could be obtained. Thus, at a committee meeting in 1944,

It was decided to enclose a slip, with the Annual Report, in the following terms: 'The Club will always welcome the offer of fish, game, poultry or fruit from any Member, and will pay full controlled prices together with the cost of carriage. Receptacles can be provided.'[15]

One member who used the club house extensively in fact comments most favourably on the quality of the food served there during the war, making special mention of his favourite cold pigeon pie.[16]

Both clubs had decided to send some of their more treasured possessions to places of safe-keeping. The Oxford and Cambridge sent 246 volumes from the library to the Bodleian, and the UUC sent the Mahoffy vase to the vaults of Drummond's Bank.* Rather late in the day, in May 1941, it was suggested that the club's wine stocks should be dispersed for safe-keeping, but no action appears to have been taken.

The real shortage which became manifest as the war went on was of wine and spirits. Wine shippers had long foreseen a war with Germany so had stocked up with hocks and Moselles. What they had not foreseen was the fall of France, so as far as burgun-

---

* Unfortunately, by the time the war ended everyone seems to have forgotten what the Mahoffy vase was. Enquiries with the Drummond's Archivist fifty years later have, perhaps unsurprisingly, thrown no light on the matter, so no-one now knows what became of it.

An old photograph of the morning room, O&C

dies and clarets were concerned they could not be replaced. At Suffolk Street in February 1943 the sale of red wines had to be restricted to the odd days of each month. At the Oxford and Cambridge the committee instructed that a slip be enclosed with the annual accounts stating that they would be willing to buy wines from members, particularly claret, in large or small quantities.

Both clubs suffered, too, from the general shortage of spirits, most of which went for export. At Suffolk Street in March 1942 the committee found it necessary to close the cocktail bar (a very recent innovation which had only started in 1940): also 'It was decided that until further notice no whisky be sold in the Club House before 5.30 p.m., and then not more than one large portion per day to each person'.[17] By 1945 they were down to single measures only. Less easy to explain, because one would have thought that ample supplies for drinking in the 1940s and 1950s would have been laid down long before the war, was the great port drought at the Oxford and Cambridge. As early as 1942 the committee had to introduce a 'points' system – each member was entitled to five small glasses a week (later reduced to three and then to twelve monthly): by 1945 it was decreed 'that not more than two bottles of port may be opened on any day, including Sunday, and for the purpose of this requirement the day shall commence at 7 p.m.'[18] Only for VE day itself did the committee relax this fearful regimen and remove all restrictions on the sale of wines and spirits.

Many members of both clubs found themselves in the uniform of one or other of the armed services during the war. Twenty-seven members of the UUC lost their lives, including one member of the Home Guard, killed on duty. Of Oxford and Cambridge members, forty-two died, including the Duke of Kent, an honorary member since 1938.

So the clubs emerged from another war, much less scarred by it than much of the rest of London, but like London, rather shabby and down-at-heel after nearly six years of no redecoration and only minimal maintenance. Arthur Kellas, a member at the Oxford and Cambridge, catches the moment vividly in his war memoirs: in 1943 he took a French acquaintance

The O&C's 'sombre coffee room', before the war

to my club in Pall Mall, which he found admirably British: that sombre coffee room, those well-worn sofas and threadbare carpets, the melancholy portraits, the empurpled bishop drinking sherry with the haggard Under-Secretary of State.[19]

The clubs had survived the war: the question now was whether they could survive its aftermath.

Notes to Chapter III

1. UUC Suggestion Book 1914
2. OC GCM, 20 October 1914
3. Quoted in John Terraine. *The First World War 1914–18*, pp. 128–9
4. OC GCM, 14 April 1915
5. NUC GCM, 21 October 1920
6. NUC GCM, 7 October 1920
7. OC GCM, 6 May 1926
8. *The Field*, 30 October 1920
9. NUC EGMM, 21 October 1919
10. NUC GCM, 6 May 1931
11. UUC GCM, 3 March 1937
12. OC GCM, 4 October 1939
13. Dr Malcolm Graeme. 'Suffolk Street in the 1940s', *Club News* No. 57 July 1988
14. Lord Wolfenden. *Turning Points*, pp. 82–3
15. UUC GCM, 26 April 1944
16. Graeme. *op. cit.*
17. UUC GCM, 12 March 1942
18. OC GCM, 2 May 1945
19. Arthur Kellas. *Down to Earth*, p. 145

Chapter IV

When Sorrows Come

In 1945 no-one really expected to see a rapid return of the golden years, though probably nobody believed that the age of austerity would continue quite as long as it did. At the Oxford and Cambridge Club there was, however, at least one notable event to mark – namely that for the first time in almost fifty years one of their members had become Prime Minister. During the war Clement Attlee had dined there regularly evening after evening. Though approachable, he was never particularly clubbable, being no conversationalist.* The committee considered how to mark the event. Rejecting the idea of a dinner and honorary membership, they decided on a portrait to be paid for by subscription. Rodrigo Moynihan was commissioned to paint it and it was hung in late 1947. Rather small-mindedly one of the committee (supported by five other members of the club) objected strenuously, demanding that his objection be minuted.

Another member of the same committee was Lt-Cdr N. S. Norway RNVR. He had read Engineering at Balliol after the first war and had then worked in the aircraft industry, first for de Havilland and later on the R100 under Barnes Wallis. During the second war he was working for the Admiralty on the design of unconventional weapons, and lived at the club for most of the

---

* As one politician put it, a conversation with an ordinary man was like a game of tennis, but a conversation with Attlee was like throwing biscuits to a dog – all you could get out of him was yup, yup, yup. (Wilfred Fienburgh, quoted by Denis Healey. *The Time of My Life*. Michael Joseph 1989, p. 153)

The morning room bar about twenty-five years ago
The portrait is of Clement Attlee, by Rodrigo Moynihan

war. Under the pseudonym of Nevil Shute he attained considerable success as a popular novelist in the 1940s and 1950s: several of his best-known novels were in fact written in the club: *Pied Piper, Most Secret* and *Pastoral*. *Pied Piper* and *A Town Like Alice*, both of which reached wider audiences through being made into films or television plays, contain scenes set in the club. In October 1958 the minutes note that 'the Committee gratefully acknowledged the gift of a picture recording the writing during the war of three Nevil Shute novels in Bedroom 8, to be hung there at his request'. It is still known as the Nevil Shute Room. Commander Norway eventually retired to Australia to live on his royalties – not, as shall be seen, the last club author to do so.

In 1946 when Rayner Goddard was appointed Lord Chief Justice, the committee at Suffolk Street proposed to hold a house dinner to mark the event; but shortages were as acute and rations as tight as they had ever been. They regretfully abandoned the idea as impossible for lack of sufficient staff, food and drink.* Meanwhile, the Oxford and Cambridge's committee was valiantly trying to relieve the great port drought which still persisted there. The club cellar, it was found, contained a surplus of first-rate claret (Ch. Latour '34), whereas Grocers' Hall had a surplus of Taylor's and Cockburn's '27 port. Could not a deal perhaps be struck for four hundred bottles, on the basis of six bottles of claret to equal five bottles of port? The Grocers stuck out for nine claret to six port: the club offered twelve to ten. Eventually in February 1946 a deal was struck: twelve dozen claret for ten dozen port.† The great drought was nearly over, though the '27 would not really be at its best for another ten years. In the interim the members would have to make do with unlimited supplies of tawny. Rationing the vintage port did not end until May 1953.

Despite the austerities the clubs did what they could to revive

---

* An attempt to relieve at any rate the shortage of staff had been made as soon as the war ended in August 1945 by an approach to the Ulster Club to see if it would be possible to recruit staff from Northern Ireland – with what degree of success is not recorded.
† Which party could be said to have got the better of the deal depends simply on whether one happens to prefer port or claret. To anyone who likes both equally it would seem that both parties had done pretty well.

the practices of peacetime: in 1946 members at the Oxford and Cambridge were asked to contribute one or two of their clothing coupons to enable the club to replace worn-out liveries. At Suffolk Street in the same year the pre-war practice of entertaining the crews to dinner after the Boat Race was revived: two years later the tradition of running a club coach to Twickenham for the 'Varsity Match was resumed and in 1951 the club again started (this time jointly with the Oxford and Cambridge) the pleasant practice of taking two boxes at Lord's for the Oxford and Cambridge match. The innovation in the following year of hiring a steamer for the Boat Race did not really catch on: demand was slight and eventually the bulk of the 160 tickets had to be off-loaded to members at the Oxford and Cambridge, the Travellers' and the United Service Clubs. Both clubs, though, made a great effort to herald what was being referred to by some as the new Elizabethan age by erecting stands for the coronation.

Certainly the most important step by either club at this time was taken at an Extraordinary General Meeting at the Oxford and Cambridge Club in January 1951 when it was decided (130 votes to 2) to acquire the adjoining house, No. 77, to serve as a ladies' annex. This house has a long and somewhat complicated history: though its present façade is mid-Victorian, there had been a house on the site since the seventeenth century, and on several occasions it has been incorporated into or separated from No. 78 next door. Some time between 1725 and 1750 No. 77 was rebuilt (it was described in 1779 as a substantial brick building with offices behind). In 1862 the lease was taken by the second Marquess of Ailesbury, who already owned No. 78, by the terms of which he was to spend not less than £6,000 in the following two years on repairing and improving No. 77 and converting No. 77 and 78 into one house. The architect employed was T. H. Wyatt,* and the new house included a ballroom, first used on 10 March 1863 to celebrate the marriage of the Prince of Wales. The entrance was through No. 78. However, when Lord Ailesbury

* Thomas Henry Wyatt (1807–80), one of a numerous clan of architects of that name. He specialised in churches, hospitals, barracks and country houses, many of them in Wales.

died, the Dowager Marchioness divided it back into two houses, a separate door being cut into the front of No. 77. This time the architect employed was Henry Curzon of Lincoln's Inn Fields. When Lady Ailesbury died in 1892 she bequeathed both her houses to her nephew, Viscount de Vesci. In 1900 the leases were bought by the Office of Works and the houses were offered to the Crown as a grace-and-favour residence, the two properties being once again reconverted into one.

In 1902 by Royal Warrant the house was granted to Queen Victoria's daughter, Princess Helena who, on marrying Prince Christian of Schleswig-Holstein, became known as Princess Christian. It was known at this time as de Vesci House but in 1906 the name was for some reason changed to Schomberg House, thereby causing ineradicable confusion with Nos 80–82 which are also called Schomberg House. On the death of Princess Christian in 1923 the house was assigned to her daughters, Princess Helena Victoria and Princess Marie Louise. In her memoirs Princess Marie Louise recalled that

My sister and I then lived at Schomberg House. It had – and I suppose still has – the most beautiful *salon* stretching the whole depth of the house from Pall Mall to Marlborough House. The lovely room possessed the most marvellous acoustics, and many of the leading artists who sang to us there said that they almost preferred it to Covent Garden.[1]

Tea at five-thirty, followed by an hour's music was the form their *soirées* took, with about fifty guests. Frieda Leider, the Wagnerian soprano, Lauritz Melchior, Friedrich Schorr and Léon Goosens all contributed. But it is to be feared that their hostess was always slightly confused about where she was living, since Professor (Sir Albert) Richardson, the President of the Royal Academy, while conducting her round some exhibition there, delivered her a potted history – but of the wrong Schomberg House. Presumably no-one liked to disabuse her of the belief that her *soirées* were taking place in the house where Thomas Gainsborough had painted. The confusion even extended to her publisher who printed in her memoirs a drawing, likewise, of the wrong Schomberg House.

1 *The United University Club, as rebuilt by Sir Reginald Blomfield*
   Watercolour by Sykes

2 *Façade of the Oxford and Cambridge Club, at the time of its completion*
Watercolour by R.Sibley, 1840

3 *The Oxford and Cambridge Club*
Watercolour by W. Walcot

4 *The smoking room*

5 *The South Library*

6 *The vestibule*

The Rev. Montague Taylor, Chairman of the O & C in the nineteenth century
The portrait by W.W.Ouless, in the coffee room

8 *The Ex-Chairmen's and Trustees' dinner, 1991*

Present: 1. *Sir Brian Cubbon*, 2. *B.R.Holland*, 3. *D.H.Conran*, 4. *Sir Robin Ibbs*, 5. *T.A.Clayton*, 6. *J.F.Phillips*, 7. *M.A.Kaye*, 8. *Sir Derek Hodgson*, 9. *D.Ll.Morgan*, 10. *J.A.Hutchings*, 11. *W.J.M.Borthwick*, 12. *J.A.Posford*, 13. *B.O.B.Williams*, 14. *C.Gunnery*, 15. *S.Matthews*, 16. *C.I.Bostock*, 17. *Sir Alec Atkinson*

The house was damaged during the Second World War: when it was finally vacated in 1947 the Chairman of the Oxford and Cambridge Club discussed with the Crown Commissioners the possibility of acquiring an option on it. They replied that the Ministry of Works would be in occupation for a few years, but that it would not be disposed of without consulting the committee. This was by no means the first occasion on which the club had shown an interest. As far back as 1860 the committee had enquired of the lessee (one Eduard Sanford) whether and on what terms he would be willing to sell the remainder of his lease. In 1878 and again in 1892 after the death of Lady Ailesbury negotiations had been opened, but on both occasions the idea had been negatived at Annual General Meetings by large majorities.[2] Another attempt was made in 1899 but foundered upon the fact that the Office of Woods and Forests was unhelpful about extending the lease to make it coterminous with that of No. 71.

The club's decision to go ahead with the purchase of No. 77 in 1951,* despite the fact that it could only be financed by overdraft, was taken very much with an eye to the future: the possibility of amalgamation at some future date with another club (perhaps the United University) was on the cards: in the meantime it would provide a very useful annex for lady associates and, on the upper floors, accommodation for staff, thereby making it possible to dispose of the staff hostel in Pimlico. Even if nothing came of the amalgamation proposal, the lease would be likely to prove a valuable investment which could always be disposed of. As things eventually turned out, their investment provided a godsend: without it, the present club would be impossibly congested – indeed, it would seem unlikely that amalgamation could ever have taken place on this site at all.

When *Spycatcher* was published in America (though not in Britain) in 1987, members were mildly astonished to discover that in the 1960s the Oxford and Cambridge Club had apparently become the favoured watering-hole of MI5. The author, Peter

* Nos 77 and 78 were thus yet again separated, No. 78 going to the Eagle Star Insurance Company.

Wright, himself a member, describes how, having spent a day interrogating a colleague suspected of spying for the Russians, he repaired to the club with his two fellow-interrogators for a recuperative drink. Within minutes, in walked the subject of their interrogation – also a member – for an exactly similar purpose. * Apart from the nice irony of members of the same club investigating each other the incident has no particular significance beyond reminding us that with the passage of time the professions and occupations of members, though not necessarily their backgrounds, tend to change. A comparison between the candidates' lists of the 1930s and the 1950s does not display much difference: candidates tend to be drawn predominantly from the traditional middle-class occupations such as barristers, solicitors, academics, physicians, engineers, clergy (though diminishingly) and civil servants (increasingly): the only significant addition to the list by 1950 is those describing themselves as company directors. By 1970, however, a whole crop of new middle-class occupations clearly emerges. Though the academics, lawyers and civil servants still hold their own, their ranks are now joined at the top of the list by bankers, chartered accountants, journalists and broadcasters, stockbrokers and management consultants. Though not so numerous, other new occupations not hitherto known to candidates' lists have begun to appear, such as computer analysts, marketing managers, account executives and business analysts. These were the green sprigs of that revival of middle-class prosperity which was to characterise the 1970s and 1980s.

Unfortunately this phenomenon did not occur in time to restore the fortunes of the clubs, which in the 1950s and 1960s reached their lowest ebb. The decline was not of course confined to the university clubs: all suffered and some went under altogether, never to resurface. Most struggled on as best they could, postponing maintenance work or living on capital, but the struggle began by the end of the 1960s to seem unwinnable. In 1971 a gloomy article in the *Financial Times* quoted one club

---

* It should perhaps be added that the member in question was completely exonerated and went on to be MI5's Director-General. Peter Wright retired to Australia.

secretary as predicting that within five years 50% of them would
have to close.[3] At both university clubs the symptoms of decline
could easily be discerned – falling membership and declining
usage. Just before the war the amalgamation at Suffolk Street of
the United University and the New University Clubs had of
course significantly boosted the membership to unprecedented
size. In the first year of peace, the club still had 1,730: but thereafter the decline appeared almost ineluctable. By 1950 it was
down only slightly to 1,723, but by 1955 it was 1,622, by 1960
1,518 and ten years later the members numbered only 1,375.
Numbers held up better at the Oxford and Cambridge, and the
acquisition of No. 77 had naturally made possible a considerable
expansion in the number of lady associates. Nevertheless, usage
as measured by the number of meals served, was going down and
down. In 1964, the committee noted, it was down by 3,000 on
the previous year, and the decline continued.* The story was
much the same at Suffolk Street, where in 1967 'members noted,
with much regret, the continued trend of insufficient usage of the
Club's facilities'.[4]

    In consequence, deficits mounted. As early as 1954 the Chair-
man of the United University Club had pointed out the serious-
ness of the club's financial position – it was losing money at the
rate of about £500 a month. A great effort was made and by the
end of the decade the position was more satisfactory and the
accounts showed a surplus of £2,600.[5] But by the mid-1960s the
club was again in difficulties and 'it was noted with regret that the
financial position continued to show a downward trend'.[6] By late
1966 the overdraft at the bank had reached £20,000. A year later it
was reported that ten members were planning to resign, fearing
that if the club collapsed financially they would be liable for the
debts out of their own pockets. Early in 1970 the committee
reported a loss for the previous year of £14,000 and the manager
at Drummond's, where the club had banked ever since 1821,
warned that the overdraft was reaching the limits he could sanc-

* The figures were

| 1965 | 62,728 | 1967 | 56,360 | 1969 | 50,303 |
| 1966 | 59,225 | 1968 | 52,567 | 1970 | 46,620 |

tion without obtaining his directors' approval. Things were little different at the other end of Pall Mall: by February 1961 the club's overdraft, which normally reached about £5,000 by the end of a year, had risen to £13,552. The loss on the previous year's trading had been £1,659. A decade later this had risen to £11,500. At this rate, the Chairman calculated, the club would have to close down by 1971. If it were to do so, it would still be liable for something like £50,000 in dilapidations.[7]

So much for the symptoms, but what was the diagnosis? Throughout these years there was no shortage of explanations for the reversals in club fortunes. Many would agree with those put forward by the Chairman at the UUC (N. R. Sharman) to an Extraordinary General Meeting in 1968:

... we as a members' club are doing no more than suffering from a malaise which all West End members' clubs are suffering from. There is a general rise in the cost of food. There is Selective Employment Tax which has been thrown on to us. Subject to correction I believe that cost £4,000 a year, which straight away is a dead loss to us. There is the increase in rates. There is the increased cost of repairs and redecorations. That is the position on one side. That gives us a smaller net profit, even if our income were to remain the same. But members are also suffering from the squeeze at home. A lot of them fear, if they are not already experiencing it, increased taxation. Their cost of living is going up, food and everything else. ...[8]

Other causes were adduced: that government offices and public companies now had their own (subsidised) canteens, and that members now tended to live much farther out of central London. But this had been happening over far too long a time-scale to provide a convincing explanation. What seems to underlie the declining fortunes of London clubs in this period is the fact that the middle classes had not yet brought themselves to come to terms with chronic inflation as a phenomenon to be accepted and allowed for. Between 1945 and 1970 the purchasing power of the pound had dropped by nearly two-thirds, but many middle-class incomes had not risen nearly enough to compensate: clerical and academic stipends certainly had not, and inflation-linked pensions were only just coming into vogue.

It would be quite unfair to the chairmen and committees of the day to suggest that they did nothing: on the contrary, the minutes of their meetings reveal a continuous preoccupation about how to cope with their financial difficulties, sometimes almost to the exclusion of all else. Many ingenious solutions were proposed and sometimes tried, though it must be said that many were to an extent counter-productive and a few downright ludicrous, such as the attempt at the Oxford and Cambridge Club to resolve its financial crisis by installing a one-armed bandit in the bar. *

When a club falls on hard times its options are limited. First, it can economise by cutting down or withdrawing entirely its least-used facilities. Second, it can try to boost its income by raising subscriptions and prices, or by enlisting more members either through a more vigorous recruitment campaign or by opening its doors to candidates hitherto not considered eligible. Third, it can, Micawber-like, start realising its assets in the hope that the money will keep things going till times improve or something turns up. Finally, if all these fail, it can pack up entirely or amalgamate with another club. During this difficult period both clubs considered and sometimes adopted all or most of these courses.

In the past it was the custom in both places for the club to remain open throughout the year apart from the month in the summer when they took each other in by turn. In 1955, however, the committee at Suffolk Street decided that savings could be made by closing the club on Sundays (apart from bedrooms) and over the Christmas holiday. It apparently worked, because in the following year they decided to close over Easter and, a year later, for the August Bank Holiday as well. At about the same date the Oxford and Cambridge considered closing for two weekends in three, arranging reciprocity with the UUC and the East India Club, but it is unclear whether the proposal was ever imple-

---

* In 1966. Apparently word had gone forth on the clubland grapevine that the In and Out had three, producing a net income of £1,000 a year, and the Devonshire had two and was making even more. The Oxford and Cambridge tried one for three months but, such were the unsporting propensities of its members, they then returned it since it was only making fifty shillings a week. Another expedient, considered but finally rejected by both clubs, was to re-vamp a billiard room as a Masonic temple.

mented: in view of the UUC's decision to close on Sundays it does not seem likely. Some years later, in 1962–63, the Oxford and Cambridge also decided to close for Christmas and Easter.

As early as 1951 the UUC decided that the 'new' smoking room, which had been added when the club house was extended eastwards to Whitcomb Street, must be divided from the club and sub-let for commercial purposes. Though this brought the club a rental income of £4,000 a year, it still was not enough: in May 1954 the Chairman (D. H. Mays-Smith) thought that the committee should consider sub-letting the three remaining downstairs smoking rooms, which would effectively have meant the club retreating to the upper floors.

Just after the war both clubs had raised subscriptions to twenty guineas. By 1966 this figure had doubled. But there were distinct limits to what could be achieved in this way, partly because every increase tended to produce a further crop of resignations from those who decided that they used the club too little to justify the expense or simply could no longer afford it: partly, too, because the clubs were competing with each other for members. Thus, when the Oxford and Cambridge in a bid for more members had decided in 1951 to abolish the entrance fee, the United University felt obliged to follow suit, much though it needed the income.

Just as in 1938 the New University Club had decided that there was no longer room for three Oxford and Cambridge clubs in London, so it was now beginning to seem that there was no longer room for more than one. However, for reasons which will become apparent, neither club at this stage was prepared to amalgamate with the other – not at any rate on terms which would be acceptable to the other. Instead both clubs considered alternative ways of making up numbers. One option which had been considered at Suffolk Street in 1954 was to allow in non-Oxbridge graduates and relations of members. Nothing came of it, but a decade later in 1965 a modified proposal on similar lines was considered – namely that eligibility should be extended to graduates of all universities which were in existence before the foundation of the club in 1821 (these would have included graduates of

Aberdeen, Dublin, Edinburgh, Glasgow and St Andrews). This too came to nothing. It was eventually the Oxford and Cambridge which finally took the plunge and at its 1967 Annual General Meeting decided to open its membership to non-graduates – a policy continued until 1971.

Meanwhile a kind of amalgamation fever had gripped London clubland as one after another began to feel the chill winds of inflation and soaring costs. In 1967 both university clubs carried on a flirtation with the University Women's Club which, in the United University case, almost came to fruition. The University Women had a freehold worth between £100,000 and £250,000 to dispose of, so they were a tempting catch. The committees of both clubs were happy with the idea but before the banns could be read an Extraordinary General Meeting of the UWC turned the idea down flat, which in the long run was probably a wise decision for both parties. The Oxford and Cambridge, similarly jilted, turned its mind to other possibilities and in the course of 1967 and 1968 discussions took place with a long and diverse list of other clubs – the Constitutional, the Devonshire, the Arts Club, the Travellers', the Reform, the Ski Club, the Farmers' Club, the United Service, the National, the Guards' and the Flyfishers'. Only the last came to anything: the Flyfishers moved into the upper billiard and card rooms at the Oxford and Cambridge, with the use of that club's coffee room and bars, in return for a rent of £3–4,000 a year.

Just to keep things going till a solution could be found, both clubs had started selling off their assets: in 1963 the Oxford and Cambridge sold some of its silver and the United University did likewise two years later. There too, the committee decided to sell some of its more valuable library books in 1967, realising thereby the sum of £8,500. In the same year the Oxford and Cambridge even contemplated selling off its entire library, possibly to some American university: they stopped short of anything quite so drastic but in 1968 they did sell their copy of Blake's *Illustrations of the Book of Job* for £1,300: a further sale of books at Sotheby's produced another £4,000.

As sometimes happens in life when things begin to go wrong, a series of other misfortunes, not logically connected, occur simultaneously. For example, when the UUC appointed a new secretary in 1958, he did not last long: within two years he had applied for the secretaryship at the Oxford and Cambridge, to which he was appointed. Shortly after he had left Suffolk Street it was discovered that he had made what the minutes described as 'unauthorised borrowings'. When he failed to repay them the club's solicitors were instructed to issue a default summons, though the committee eventually changed their minds, deciding to write the sum off as a bad debt. He did not last very long at the Oxford and Cambridge either: he was sacked within two years for making similar misappropriations. Again, Suffolk Street in 1965 and 1966 suffered a series of minor fires.* In 1968 at the Oxford and Cambridge there was a wages snatch in which the club suffered a loss of nearly a thousand pounds. In 1971 at Suffolk Street it was discovered that the four volumes of Ackermann's *History of Oxford and Cambridge* had had all the prints removed. All, as has been said, unconnected events, but cumulatively hardly calculated to improve committee morale.

It must be said that during these post-war decades neither club was able to present a specially enticing face to the world. The Oxford and Cambridge Club, being by far the more costly of the two to maintain because of the palatial scale of its public rooms, became shabby and down-at-heel: one member who joined in 1958 recalls the general impression as being 'distinctly seedy'. Suffolk Street probably did better in this respect, but no-one could really enthuse about the food. Older members, conditioned by years of rationing and austerity, tended to accept things as they were but younger members, aware that in the world outside the age of austerity was over, were apt to be critical of a coffee room where it seemed still to linger. 'The standard of meals supplied', the committee conceded in 1962, 'must be greatly improved in order to counter the trend of members dining elsewhere.'[9] Six years later a young member told an EGM

---

* Not altogether unmitigated disasters since the club was able to redecorate the ladies' side out of the insurance money – something they could not otherwise have afforded.

'I eat out most of the nights of the week, but I am afraid this club does not on most occasions represent an attractive alternative to most of the other places where I might choose to eat. It is shaming if one has to apologise to one's guests for the service and food, and I am afraid one frequently does if you bring guests here.'[10] Despite, therefore, the efforts of Suffolk Street's resident members in the universities,* and the intermittent though not always vigorous attempts by the committee to recruit members there, it is not surprising that interest among the undergraduates was lukewarm: many who did join soon lost interest and resigned. There is no need to cite the prevailing political climate among students in the 1960s as a significant factor in all this, for those who were affected by it would probably never had considered joining a West End club anyway.

Still, not all was doom and gloom. During the last two years of their separate existences both clubs gave signs of revived activity. The Oxford and Cambridge mounted a Viennese ball with great success: at Suffolk Street, greatly assisted by the appointment of a new Secretary (D. J. McDougall), an overhaul of the management and catering brought a greater professionalism to the running of the club. Communication with the membership was improved by the publication of a thrice-yearly *Club Bulletin*: a quite lively series of club discussion dinners was begun with speakers such as Professor Stuart Piggott, David Butler, Peter Walker and Sir Arthur Bryant. On 20 May 1971 the club celebrated its sesquicentenary with a dinner attended by the two Chancellors (Harold Macmillan and Lord Adrian).

To a later generation who did not know either of them at first hand it will no doubt seem extraordinary that the two university clubs hesitated for so long before deciding to amalgamate. They had after all much more in common with each other than they had with any other club since they drew their members from identical backgrounds. Ever since they were established, the clubs had traditionally provided each other with hospitality during their

* Robert (later Lord) Blake, succeeded by the Reverend Leslie Styler, at Oxford: Noel (later Lord) Annan, succeeded by Glyn Daniel, at Cambridge.

annual closures. The idea that they should amalgamate was by no means novel: it will be recalled that right back in the 1830s the suggestion had been mooted that Smirke should build a club house capable of accommodating both and that this intention had only been frustrated by his inability to acquire a large enough site. During the First World War, fearing that as the universities had been so denuded of undergraduates there might not be an adequate supply of future candidates, the chairmen of all three university clubs had met to discuss the possibility of amalgamation. In 1954 the two chairmen had discussed a possible merger, retaining both houses, one with a much reduced staff and cafeteria meals, the other with higher prices and the best of everything (ah, but which?).[11] In spring 1966 both clubs had made a real effort and a meeting between some committee members and the chairmen of both clubs discussed their joint futures and a possible amalgamation, perhaps in new premises. A joint committee dinner took place in July, but again led to no decision.

In January 1967 the committee at the Oxford and Cambridge took professional advice from Messrs Jones Lang Wootton, who told them that if the two clubs were to amalgamate it would have to be at 71 Pall Mall because No. 71 was unusable as anything but a club and the lease expressly prohibited a different use, whereas Suffolk Street's lease was less stringent and the club house was more adaptable. But so far as the UUC was concerned, that was the sticking point: in February the Chairman wrote to the Oxford and Cambridge rejecting amalgamation on such terms. It had been this – apparently final – rejection which had led the Oxford and Cambridge into that great flurry of negotiations with other clubs and eventually to the decision to open its doors to non-graduates.

The fact was that both clubs were deeply attached to their own very different houses and could not bear the idea of having to abandon one for the other. If this seems petty-minded, just think what the reaction would have been to any suggestion that Christ Church, say, should amalgamate with Magdalen on the other's site, or Trinity with King's.

The United University Club's resolution was somewhat weak-

ened in May 1967 when it received a letter from the Crown
Commissioners advising it that no major capital expenditure
should be made since the whole area between Suffolk Street and
Whitcomb Street would be due for large-scale redevelopment in
about 1974. Even so, all did not seem lost even by the end of 1970,
for it seemed that it might be possible to surrender the unexpired
lease in exchange for new premises in Suffolk Street to the north
together with a *douceur* of £10,000 with the possibility of more.
The Crown Commissioners appointed Sir Hugh Casson consultant architect for the redevelopment of the whole peninsular site
between Suffolk Street and Whitcomb Street. 'Once accommodated in a labour-saving, purpose-built Club House, the Committee is confident we can continue for another hundred and fifty
years.'[12]

In September 1970 the committee at the Oxford and Cambridge were advised that time was running out: at the present rate
of loss the club would have to close at the end of 1971. Over the
next few months several ideas were considered. One was to sell
No. 77, the ladies' annex: another was a merger with the United
Service Club (in that house): a third was the possibility of
redeveloping a part of the club house as flats. In November 1970
there was a further meeting of the management committee of the
two university clubs at which the Chairman of the UUC (C. F.
Thring) proposed that the two clubs should move into No. 71
while the new club house was being built after which they could
move back to Suffolk Street permanently. A committee of four
was set up to pursue the matter.

However, it all looked far from certain, and early in 1971 the
Chairman of the Oxford and Cambridge (T. A. Clayton) wrote
to all members calling an Extraordinary General Meeting to wind
up the club and to propose amalgamation with the United Service
Club. Rumours that the club was in difficulties had by now
reached the national press: when it met in late January the
UUC's general committee expressed concern about an article
which had appeared in *The Times* about the probable closure of
the Oxford and Cambridge Club and the anticipated removal of
some five hundred of its members to the United Service Club.

Then, in May 1971 two things happened. First, at an Extraordinary General Meeting the committee's resolution to wind up the Oxford and Cambridge Club was negatived (for 105, against 157).[13] This was immediately followed by the Annual General Meeting, at which the entire general committee resigned (though some members who had opposed winding up were re- elected).[14] The second thing was that the general committee at Suffolk Street was informed that since the Trafalgar Square development was to incorporate a massive extension of the National Gallery, it now seemed extremely unlikely that any part of the Suffolk Street-Whitcomb Street site would be available for a new club house. Any chance, therefore, of an amalgamation there was a dead duck. It really did seem as if the United University Club had celebrated its hundred-and-fiftieth anniversary only just in the nick of time.

Notes to Chapter IV

1. Princess Marie Louise. *My Memories of Six Reigns*, p. 208
2. OC GCM, 14 December 1860; OC AGMM 1878 and 1891
3. 'The quiet crisis in clubland', *Financial Times*, 23 February 1971
4. UUC GCM, 27 September 1967
5. UUC GCM, 25 February 1959 and 29 June 1960
6. UUC GCM, 27 July 1966
7. OC GCM, 6 January 1971
8. UUC EGMM, 14 February 1968
9. UUC GCM, 28 November 1962
10. UUC EGMM, 14 February 1968
11. UUC GCM, 1 September 1954
12. UUC *Club Bulletin* No. 2 September 1970
13. OC EGMM and AGMM 11 May 1971
14. UUC GCM, 17 May 1971.

Chapter V

The Maiden Phoenix

The reluctance on the part of both university clubs to do what must have seemed to any detached observer the obvious thing and join forces can at any rate in part be explained by that gentle rivalry between them, usually jocular and good-humoured, not unlike that between the two universities themselves, but which can sometimes veer towards bloody-mindedness and acrimony when provoked by personality or circumstance. When the two committees had dined together in November 1970, for reasons not entirely clear and which are probably best left unexplored, they had not hit it off: both continued to seek other solutions to their problems. At Suffolk Street the committee began looking for another home when it became clear that they could not for long stay where they were: 5 St James's Square, 18 Carlton House Terrace, the Devonshire Club – even 71 Pall Mall should the Oxford and Cambridge be forced eventually to wind up – were all considered. The Oxford and Cambridge's committee, it was reported, were involved in talks with the Devonshire, the Public Schools and the National Liberal Clubs, though they would still be prepared to welcome the UUC at 71 Pall Mall or elsewhere.[1]

The apparently quixotic decision by the members at their Extraordinary General Meeting in May 1971 to overrule the Oxford and Cambridge committee's recommendation to call it a day appears to have been decisively influenced by the former Chairman of the New University Club, Colonel Burrow Hill: he was a member of both the UUC and the Oxford and Cambridge. Acting purely on his own initiative he urged members to hang on because he was convinced that in the end the United University would come round and agree to amalgamation.

Fortunately, he was right. Since February it had appeared that Coutts & Co., in need of a temporary home while their head office was rebuilt, might be interested in taking the twenty-eight years of the Suffolk Street lease: since August a deal had been worked out whereby the two existing leases on 71 and 77 Pall Mall could be surrendered and might be replaced by a 60-year ground rent without rent reviews. The result was a sum of £350,000 in the hands of UUC members, a substantial contribution towards the work at Pall Mall, the avoidance of a hefty dilapidation claim and, as an added bonus, a considerable saving in Capital Gains Tax.

This offer transformed the situation. The main snag to amalgamating with the Oxford and Cambridge Club at 71 Pall Mall had been that, in its by now decrepit and unattractive state, it would need a great deal of money spending on it to make it a habitable and fitting home for a united club. Now, with such a substantial dowry in prospect, the United University could re-open negotiations, this time very much on its own terms. The Chairman, James Bishop, wasted little time: on 16 September he wrote to the Chairman of the Oxford and Cambridge Club setting them out. It is a letter of such importance that it is worth quoting in full.

PRIVATE & CONFIDENTIAL

September 16, 1971.

Judge Figgis
Chairman
Oxford & Cambridge University Club
71 Pall Mall
London S.W.1.

Dear Judge Figgis,

As you know, the plans for redeveloping the United University Club's premises on our present site have fallen through because of the announced desire of the National Gallery and National Portrait

Gallery ultimately to extend their premises across Whitcomb Street and into our site. Faced with the fact that we can no longer look forward as a club to an assured future on our present site my committee has decided to recommend to the members acceptance of an offer from Coutts Bank for our leasehold interest in the Suffolk Street property. Letters of agreement have been exchanged, and as a result the United University Club will shortly have to decide where it wishes to re-establish itself.

We are now fortunately in a sound financial position to do this because the offer from Coutts is a substantial one. Naturally, UUC members will expect our committee to look at all the possibilities that are now open to us, and this we have done and are doing. However, the experience of recent years both of our own club and of yours convinces us that in today's circumstances there can in the long run only be one viable club in London composed basically of graduates from Oxford and Cambridge. Because of this, and knowing that the Oxford & Cambridge University Club is like ourselves seeking a realistic basis on which to secure its future, my committee believes that the best way forward would be to reunite the two clubs.

Accordingly I am writing now on behalf of my committee to propose reunification along the following lines:–

1. That the two clubs should be reconstituted as one club composed of the present members of both clubs.

2. That the house for the reconstituted club should be the present site, including ladies' annexe, of the Oxford & Cambridge University Club in Pall Mall.

3. That these premises should be renovated and provided with new and improved facilities in accordance with plans to be put forward by the present United University Club, to be paid for with money provided by that Club.

4. That the lease of the Oxford & Cambridge premises shall be surrendered to the Crown, who will by prior agreement then grant a new and longer lease to the reconstituted club at a nominal annual rent with no rent revisions, the annual rent being considerably lower than your present rent. We believe we would be able to negotiate such an arrangement with the Crown as part of the deal for vacating our premises and moving to yours.

5. That the reconstituted club at Pall Mall should be called the United University Club.

6. That the date for occupation by the reconstituted club of its redeveloped premises should be January 1, 1973, and that prior to this date while work is being carried out members will live in the present premises of the UUC.

7. That the date for establishing the reconstituted club should be not later than March 1, 1972, and that the two clubs shall join together in the Suffolk Street premises on or before that date.

8. That the first committee of the reconstituted club which shall remain in office for not less than one year from the date of formation of the club, shall be composed of two-thirds UUC members and one-third Oxford & Cambridge University Club members, with a chairman drawn from the UUC. Subsequent committees will be by election of the reunited club and will not be subject to any such arrangement.

9. That this committee should be formed before the end of 1971 and charged with the task of drawing up new rules for the reconstituted club and other plans for the amalgamation.

10. That a smaller committee of six composed of three members from each club under the chairmanship of the United University Club chairman with the Oxford & Cambridge University Club chairman as deputy chairman shall be formed immediately to make all necessary preparations for the change and to make arrangements for securing the necessary approval of the membership of the two clubs.

11. That the secretaries of the two clubs shall be retained, the United University Club secretary to serve as the general secretary and the Oxford & Cambridge University Club secretary as membership secretary of the reconstituted club.

12. That these heads of agreement, when agreed by the general committee of both clubs, shall be put before extraordinary general meetings of the full memberships of both clubs which shall be separately called to obtain their agreement before the end of 1971.

I have set out our proposals with some precision because, as you know, our two clubs have been involved in a number of attempted negotiations in the past which have foundered through misunderstandings and confusions. I personally believe that the proposals I have outlined above will offer the best chance to the members of both clubs of ensuring that a club of Oxford and Cambridge men can continue to flourish in London. I am sure that is what the majority of members of both our clubs would want, and I am hopeful that they will agree that this plan offers a realistic way of bringing it about.

I look forward to hearing from you.
Yours sincerely,
James Bishop
Chairman

When things like that begin to happen they tend to happen fast: in this case they had to, for Coutts had stipulated that they wanted vacant possession of the club house on 1 January 1973 or twelve months after the exchange of contracts, whichever was the later. On 29 October 1971 the management committee of the UUC and the finance committee of the Oxford and Cambridge Club met and agreed in principle to amalgamate: both clubs would put the detailed proposals to their general committees and ultimately to meetings of the clubs' full memberships before the end of the year. At simultaneous EGMs on 1 December the members of both clubs agreed to the amalgamation. *

Much of the credit for the deal with Coutts is due to the Chairman of the UUC's redevelopment sub-committee, Eric Vallis, to whom James Bishop paid tribute in his speech at the Extraordinary General Meeting:

I fear the club will never really know the extent of its debt to Mr Vallis, who has worked tirelessly on our behalf, following up the unlikeliest of possibilities, producing scheme after scheme for the committee to examine, and finally emerging with the offer from Coutts which we have before us tonight, and which he is refining even now to reduce our tax liabilities and ensure that collectively we as members get the best possible benefit from the offer.

It was entirely fitting that in due course the new club conferred honorary membership on both James Bishop and Eric Vallis in recognition of their achievements in bringing it all about.

There were of course still a great number of i's to be dotted and t's to be crossed before contracts could be exchanged: Coutts for their part required planning consent to use the club premises for business purposes: a decision had to be reached about what to do over those non-graduates who had joined the Oxford and Cam-

---

* As a concession to the other club's *amour propre* the UUC dropped the stipulation about the name and agreed to join forces under the pantechnicon title of The United Oxford and Cambridge University Club.

bridge Club since 1967 (they were, naturally, allowed to stay, though no more were to be recruited): provision had to be made for long-serving members of staff from both clubs: the rules and regulations had to be harmonised – all hard graft for a committee few of whose members in these times could afford lives of leisure or retirement.

The committee of the new club (or, as we can henceforth call it, simply 'the club') held its first meeting at Suffolk Street on 21 December 1971: James Bishop was elected its first Chairman with Cedric Gunnery as Vice-Chairman. It was agreed that the Oxford and Cambridge Club would close its doors at the beginning of March and its members would move to Suffolk Street on 7 March 1972.* The combined membership numbered 3,460 including 526 overseas members and 563 lady associates: 2,006 came from the Pall Mall House, 1,454 from Suffolk Street. Quite apart from the Coutts money and the reduced overheads resulting from a shared club house, the boost in numbers presaged an altogether healthier financial future than either club would have faced on its own.

The move to Suffolk Street was of course no more than a holding operation: though it created logistical problems for the secretaries and staff, the fitting of a quart of members into a pint-sized club house proved easier than might have been expected. But if Coutts's deadline was to be met there was barely a year in which to carry out the alterations and repairs needed at 71 Pall Mall. Inevitably, some of the more ambitious proposals originally envisaged, such as a sauna, a swimming bath and a car park had to be dropped either for lack of money or lack of space. Squash courts,† however, of which the UUC had two but the Oxford and Cambridge none, were (or at any rate were thought

---

* The debate as to whether the clubs amalgamated in 1971 or 1972 is thus a semantic one, like whether a reign begins at the accession or the coronation: the EGMs had voted to amalgamate and the new club's committee had met in December 1971: the clubs merged physically in March 1972.

† The squash courts at Suffolk Street had been added in 1939–40. Unlike those to be added at 71 Pall Mall, they were at the top of the building instead of the bottom, and quite hard to find. As the chairman of the squash committee put it in the first *Club Bulletin*, 'the two squash courts on the roof of the building are reached by a combination of moving in a heavenly direction and luck'.

to be) indispensable for attracting young members. More bedrooms, too, were needed, and these, it was felt, must meet modern standards by having private bathrooms. All this work had to be done in an existing building with very restricted access and inflexible time limits.[2]

The architects appointed were Robert Maguire and Keith Murray of Kew Green and the builders were a medium-sized family firm, J. W. Falkner and Sons of Lambeth. Perhaps the key to the whole operation was transferring the kitchen, which had been in the basement two floors below the coffee room, to the same level as the coffee room itself, thereby releasing space in the basement and ground floor for the squash courts, changing rooms, a billiards room, a squash bar and two rooms for private functions, now known as the Marlborough and King Edward Rooms. In the basement too was an elaborate warren of wine cellars, stores, a boiler room, a maintenance workshop, a laundry room, a lift motor room, a chef's office and so on. In assembling this complicated jig-saw puzzle the committee could do no more than state its requirements and approve outline proposals: the details had to be left to the architects to work out as they went along. The task called for great ingenuity and eclecticism. For example, the squash courts, it was found, could only be fitted in by shaving away four-and-a-half inches of Smirke's weight-bearing west wall of the club house in the basement. Again, only eight feet of head-room was available in the Marlborough Room: in order to make this seem less oppressive the architects adopted the device of lowering the ceiling round the sides to make the centre appear higher. Space had also somehow to be found in the basement and ground floor for a new staff dining room and sitting room, offices for the secretaries and the accounts office (these had previously been in the area behind the porter's lodge) and a television room.

Above stairs the main public rooms were left substantially intact: the only alterations apart from fitting in the new kitchen and a new lift were to convert what had previously been the bar (originally the strangers' dining room) into a buffet/wine bar and to instal the members' bar in what had previously been known as the morning room (the previous quick luncheon room on the ground floor was now the upper part of the squash courts). All the main rooms badly needed repairing and redecorating: well knowing that whatever they did would be found fault with, the committee wisely resorted to authenticity by reverting as far as possible to Smirke's original decoration scheme.

At the upper levels the bedroom floors were virtually gutted and thirty-nine bedrooms with *en suite* bathrooms were installed instead of the previous nineteen – a conjuring trick only achieved by sacrificing the billiards and card rooms on the third floor. The outcome was not entirely satisfactory; it meant that some bedrooms ended up with only skylights instead of windows and this had to be put right later. However, bedrooms (at £5 a night plus VAT) were of such importance to the financial viability of the club that it seemed important to fit in as many as possible.

It was all a terrific scramble: the Suffolk Street club house was due to close on 9 February 1973 and 71 Pall Mall was scheduled to open on 12 March. Meanwhile, hospitality was arranged for members at fifteen other clubs. Not everything was ready: the ladies' side could not open until 24 April and the squash courts, squash bar and the first seven bedrooms were not available until October (the remaining bedrooms were promised for the end of January 1974). But somehow the near-impossible was achieved, by and large to members' general satisfaction. It had all cost £590,000.

To many who had been members of the United University Club, which had been associated with Suffolk Street for a century and a half, leaving there was a great wrench: some felt they could not manage it and resigned. But all in all the two memberships settled in most amicably, without a trace of the old rivalry which had for so long made them reluctant to unite, in the knowledge that the club had done the sensible thing and now faced a much more secure future.

This did not mean, however, that financial problems were a thing of the past. The 1970s, and to a lesser extent the 1980s, were decades of vertiginous inflation: by 1979 a pound's purchasing

Bookplates of the UUC, O&C and UOCUC

power was less than a third of what it was in 1969: by 1989 it bought only half what it had in 1979.* But by the 1970s the middle classes in general (and club committees in particular) were learning their lesson: if they were to survive, earnings and prices and subscriptions must keep step remorselessly with the rate of inflation. If members could not keep up and had to resign, that was very sad but it was unavoidable. In 1975 the full-rate subscription was £55; for 1977 it was raised to £80 and for 1978 it was £100. By 1981 it had risen to £180 and by 1982 it was £203. By the end of the decade it had doubled again. The prices of meals and drinks rose in proportion. But by now no-one could remember the days when clubs could sell wines at the laying-down price and meals virtually at cost – let alone provide free beer.

Each rise in subscriptions nevertheless brought with it a massive wave of resignations. Sometimes the reason given was 'financial' but more commonly 'lack of use', which probably came to much the same thing. The time was long gone when many members belonged to three, four, five or even more clubs, some of which they probably only visited a few times a year: now if they did that it was probably costing them a hundred pounds or more each time they entered the portals. To compensate, it was essential that the club mounted and maintained a more positive recruiting policy, both within the universities and in the wide world, and for this purpose a membership sub-committee was established which, particularly under the chairmanship of Derek Conran (a future Chairman of the club), brought to bear a vigorous – and sometimes controversial – campaign of a kind previously more familiar to the market place than the club house. It involved cocktail parties and mail-shots and advertising in the press and altogether seemed most undignified: happily, it produced results so that by the end of the 1980s elections had not just kept pace with resignations but had overtaken them. By the 1990s

---

* For purposes of comparison with earlier decades, the equivalent purchasing power of £1 in terms of its 1989 value were

1939 £26.20	1959 £9.30
1949 £13.20	1969 £6.60

(Central Office of Information figures).

the committee was seriously anticipating having to put up the 'House Full' notices.

The *Club Bulletin*, started by Boyd Bowman in the last years of the United University Club, was continued.* Browsing through its back numbers for the 1970s, one becomes aware of a gathering momentum and vitality in the life of the club since the amalgamation. Two Suffolk Street activities – wine tastings and discussion dinners – have become firmly established institutions: wine tastings, which served to introduce members to the whole range of the club's still estimable cellar, proved particularly popular with younger members. For the discussion dinners speakers were sometimes drawn from the club's membership, such as Sir John Wolfenden, General Sir John Hackett, Lord Blake and Stuart Piggott, and sometimes from without, such as Lord Whitelaw, Kingman Brewster (then United States Ambassador in London), Shirley Williams, Sir Hugh Casson and Caspar Weinberger. Some filled the coffee room, while others, attracting smaller numbers, could be held in the more intimate setting of the Marie Louise Room (formerly the ladies' dining room) where true discussion could take place rather than a question-and-answer session.

Celebrating public occasions – an old Oxford and Cambridge Club tradition – also continued. In 1981, to mark the fortieth anniversary of the Grand Alliance, an Anglo-American dinner was held jointly with the Harvard and Yale Clubs in London, with General Bernard Rogers (the Supreme Allied Commander in Europe) and Sir Leon Brittan (Chief Secretary to the Treasury) as guests of honour. Earlier in the same year the club celebrated, both on the eve and on the day itself, the marriage of the Prince of Wales (an honorary member since 1970) to Lady Diana Spencer with champagne, a dinner, an orchestra from the band of the Royal Artillery and an entertainment by Bernard Miles. Other celebrations were of a more private nature, such as the dinner arranged for Selwyn Lloyd as Speaker of the House of Commons

---

* In 1982 the title was changed to *Club News*. When Boyd Bowman died in 1981 the editorship had passed to Denis Moylan and, on his retirement in 1983, to its present editor, Michael Hill.

Harold Macmillan (later 1st Earl of Stockton) at the Chancellors' dinner

in 1975, for King Olav of Norway (the club's senior honorary member) in 1979 and Chancellors' dinners in 1975 (for Harold Macmillan and Lord Adrian) and in 1987 (for the Duke of Edinburgh and Lord Jenkins). In 1988 a dinner was planned to mark the hundred-and-fiftieth anniversary of the club house.

Two innovations which proved extremely popular, the former invariably being fully booked within a few days of its announcement, were the Christmas dinner, ending with entertainment by the Players' Theatre and carols round the Christmas tree, and the St Valentine's Day dinner, ending with madrigals and red roses for the ladies. Other ventures which proved less successful were a debate (only one was held, on the motion 'That the Universities of Oxford and Cambridge are a desirable anachronism'), and musical evenings: one, provided, by the Arditti String Quartet, was not well attended – possibly because it took place on a Sunday evening – and there seems to have been no successor. The only surviving musical event in the club's calendar is the annual concert provided by the Oxford and Cambridge Musical Club. Perhaps the most ambitious venture was a club ball in 1979, attended by 623 members and guests, with dancing in the coffee room, a disco in the Marlborough Room and the Cambridge Footlights performing in the squash courts: though greatly enjoyed by those who attended, it proved a mammoth operation involving the closure of the club for four days and the over-night evacuation of much of the club furniture in pantechnicons to St James's Square. It made a trading loss of £2,197 to which had to be added a further £1,000 in lost revenue, and was felt to be too disruptive an operation to be repeated except on rare and special occasions.[3] Still, this plethora of activities did much to bring the club to life, possibly as never before.* To exemplify the scale of these activities it is only necessary to look at the programme for a single quarter – as it happens, the last three months of 1986. This read:

Real Ale and English Cheese Tasting
Literary Dinner (Jonathan Raban)
Discussion Dinner (Lord Hailsham)
Members' Claret Tasting
Gourmets' Grouse Dinner
Discussion Dinner (Michael Bloch)
Members' Christmas Dinner

---

* Not, needless to say, to every member's satisfaction: as one elderly member was overheard to complain to another, 'This used to be a nice quiet club. Now they're for ever holding balls and dinners and cocktail parties and all sorts of *jollifications*'.

As the new Chairman (Christopher Bostock) summed it up in his Chairman's Notes, 'As I look back through the recent notes of my fluent predecessor, I see a picture of a busy, prosperous club, ever mixing new activities among the traditional ones and trying to keep up with changing tastes. I hope it will continue this way.'[4]

Another direction in which the club greatly expanded its activity in the years since amalgamation was in the establishment of reciprocal arrangements with other (mainly university) clubs overseas. It had for many years been the practice of both clubs to have such arrangements with a handful of others, but these had mainly been with provincial clubs in the United Kingdom (many of which have subsequently withered and died): only two were with clubs abroad and these were in Europe. None existed with clubs in the United States. Since 1972 the list had gradually grown to nearly a hundred: twenty-five in Europe (including the United Kingdom), nine in Africa, ten in Australia and New Zealand, eleven in the Far East and forty in the Americas – thereby providing members with a worldwide alternative to the Sheratons and Intercontinentals should they wish to make use of it.

In some respects it has taken the club longer to come right than in others. Competing as it has to with hotels and restaurants for staff, to secure and retain the services of men and women of the right calibre has always proved a headache for the Secretary. To alleviate the problem the committee decided once again to acquire a staff hostel. After one or two abortive attempts a suitable building was found (50 West Cromwell Road) in 1980 to house sixteen staff. The freehold was acquired for £90,000 including professional fees (though in the end it cost £80,000 more because of all the fire, health and safety regulations which had to be met).[5] How far it succeeded in achieving its object in debatable, since the high turnover of staff continues to be a problem. However, as a sound investment in a rising property market and as a way of releasing more bedroom accommodation in the club house itself for members, there was undoubtedly much to be said for it.

Mention has already been made of the depressing and sometimes dire quality of the cuisine in both clubs in the years preceding the amalgamation. To begin with, things were not much better in the united club: though the kitchen could always rise to some special occasion, the routine food in the coffee room remained dreary until the appointment of Chef Morrison in 1978. *
This coincided with the appointment of a new coffee room manager (Woods) and between the two the quality of the food and service improved sensationally. Previously the coffee room, which like most clubs did fair business at lunchtimes, had been almost deserted at dinner. Now, as the word gradually spread, the room began to do as well if not better in the evening as it did at lunchtime, particularly when, at the beginning of 1981, last orders were extended until nine o'clock instead of half-past eight. Already in December 1980 the Secretary had been able to report to the committee 'that the month's profit of £11,347 is a record ... This is largely due to the month's increased meal usage of 11% on last year, which is a reflection of the excellence of the Chef'.[6] In the June 1983 issue of *Decanter* the club was accorded a further accolade: 'Lunch, in which the United Oxford and Cambridge Club proved itself in a class of its own among the clubs, also confirms how well traditional English food shows off good wine'.[7]

So at last the food was able to match the quality of the cellar which, it had been comfortingly reported in 1975, contained sufficient reserves of vintage port for twenty-two years, vintage claret (mainly '66 and '70) for nine years and vintage red burgundy for five years. Three years later the Secretary reported more specifically to the management committee that the club's vintage wine stocks stood at the levels set out overleaf – and this to meet an average annual consumption (based on the previous four years) of some two thousand bottles of vintage wine:

---

* His predecessor had finally been dismissed after a third formal warning after serving roast turkey to a private function complete with the giblets inside in a plastic bag. Even so, it took an Industrial Tribunal a five-day sitting to confirm that he had not been unfairly dismissed.

Claret	24,692 bottles
Red Burgundy	4,651 bottles
Port	12,664 bottles[8]

Now that the club had achieved financial stability it was possible to do something about those other aspects of its activities which had for so long been neglected: the last of those threadbare carpets and well-worn sofas were replaced, and the library was able to resume a proper purchasing and conservation policy: during the ten years beginning in 1981 over 1,200 new books were added to the existing stock. Suitable long-term provision under a twenty-five year plan could be made for major repairs and refurbishment, a completely new, stainless steel roof could be installed and, by no means least, the lease on the club house was extended until well into the second half of the twenty-first century.

To what are we to attribute this almost sensational recovery in the club's fortunes since the amalgamation? Basically, it would seem, to the reviving middle-class fortunes of the 1970s and, particularly, of the 1980s. As salaries (and, perhaps, expense accounts) rose and punitive taxation was substantially diminished, the middle classes started remembering how to enjoy themselves. But that in itself would not have been sufficient: what was also required was a greatly enhanced professionalism and much enthusiasm and hard work at both managerial and secretarial levels. The 1970s and 1980s had required cool heads and steady nerves to cope with endemic inflation, soaring subscriptions and the consequent harvests of resignations. At times it must have been difficult to remember always to look up-market, never down. The club has been fortunate in its secretaries and chairmen since amalgamating, some of whom, such as Robert Holland and Bruce Williams, have devoted unceasing energy and expertise, both in office and out of it, to the taxing task of keeping the club financially sound. The future is always fraught with the menace of the contingent and the unforeseen. If in the future the club should be caught out by it, it will not have been their fault.

Notes to Chapter V

1. UUC GCM, 21 July 1971
2. Most of the information about these works is drawn from an undated galley proof by various hands in the club archives. The relevant section of it was written by the Chairman, James Bishop
3. UOCUC GCM, 7 November 1979
4. *Club News* No. 51 July 1986
5. UOCUC Management Committee Minutes, 30 April 1980
6. UOCUC GCM, 3 December 1980
7. Quoted in *Club News* No. 43 November 1983
8. UOCUC Management Committee Minutes, 25 October 1978

Chapter VI

The Way We Lived Then

Anyone examining the club's archives is likely to reach the conclusion that, while human nature changes not at all, the customs and requirements of clubs and their members have altered a good deal. There are continuities, of course: to be eligible for election a candidate must still have attended one or other of the ancient universities, and any founder member of the Oxford and Cambridge Club returning to his old haunts would quickly recognise his surroundings – the morning room, the smoking room, the North and South Libraries (though he might well be taken aback to find strangers and ladies eating in the coffee room). He might even find among the members' list family names whose grandfathers or great-grandfathers he had known, and on the shelves in the libraries books which he had read. But much else would be different, which prompts the question of how and in what ways the clubs, when founded, differed in their objects and function from the club as we know it today. More broadly, what light is shed by the clubs and their members on the social history of the nineteenth and twentieth centuries? The question seems worth asking because for many years the writing of the social history of this period was dominated by the 'condition of the people' question: the rise to dominance of what in the early nineteenth century was referred to as the 'middling class' has been comparatively neglected. If much of what follows seems to be concerned with their quirks and foibles, it is worth remembering that these can eloquently express their underlying values and attitudes.

The Members

The proliferation of London clubs – and even as early as 1837 *The Monthly Magazine* identified twenty-eight of them as opposed to the mere half-dozen or so dating from the eighteenth century[1] – seems to have been the result of two trends, both gathering momentum as the century proceeded. One was the growing dominance of London in the nation's affairs: the other was the determination of an expanding middle class to consolidate its position.

It will be recalled that of the five moving spirits in the foundation of the United University Club, four were Members of Parliament and the fifth was Chaplain to the House of Commons. Before the railways came, travel was expensive, uncomfortable and mightily slow.* It was understandable, therefore, that country members absented themselves from Westminster for weeks and even months at a time. Yet from about 1820 public opinion, led by Joseph Hume's speeches and pamphlets, was putting pressure on them to attend more regularly. They needed somewhere to eat and relax when Parliament was sitting since, before Sir Charles Barry's sumptuous new building was completed in 1852, all the Palace of Westminster had to offer by way of refreshment was the snack bar established there by John Bellamy (of veal pie fame) in 1773. Thus it was that the United University Club came to be regarded 'as above all things the London home of the country gentlemen in the Commons'.[2]

With the arrival of the railways and the electric telegraph in the 1830s and 1840s, spinning the great web of which London was the centre, it became desirable – even necessary – for gentlemen to establish for themselves a London base, whereas in earlier times their preoccupations had been purely local. In Jane Austen's England London was impossibly distant and the country gentry scarcely ever want there: by Trollope's day, the railway had reached Barchester and the Bishop Proudies and Archdeacon Grantlys were for ever rushing to and fro. The railways in turn

---

* By fastest mail-coach in 1800 the journey from Bristol to London took sixteen hours. In 1834, when Wellington recommended William IV to send for Peel to form a ministry, Peel was in Rome: it would take a month to bring him back.

enhanced the importance of the London-based national press (*The Jupiter* was after all *the* power in Barchester's affairs), thereby supplanting the importance of the local capitals in the counties. With ecclesiastical affairs so frequently to the fore in nineteenth-century politics, it is no surprise that so many of the clergy, who formed such a substantial section of the university clubs' memberships, came from the country despite the fact that country members received no concession in the matter of subscriptions.

In the preamble to its original rules the Oxford and Cambridge Club proclaimed itself to have been 'instituted for the association of gentlemen educated at those universities, and for promoting and continuing a mutual interest and fellowship between them'. The unspoken assumption behind the phrase appears to be not that only gentlemen who had been educated there were eligible but rather that the very fact of having been educated there conferred on them the status of gentlemen. Here was an extension to the meaning of the word which earlier generations would not have considered. 'You misled me by the term gentleman,' says Sir Walter Elliott in Jane Austen's *Persuasion*. 'I thought you were speaking of some man of property.' That was 1818; but as late as 1875 there are Trollopian echoes:

There are no doubt gentlemen of different degrees, but the English gentleman of gentlemen was he who had land, and family title-deeds, and an old family place, and family portraits, and family embarrassments, and a family absence of any usual employment.[3]

However, the extension of the term is symbolic: by the nineteenth century the educated professional middle classes were seeking greater dignity and exclusiveness – hence the formation in this period of professional associations such as the Royal College of Surgeons (1800), the Institution of Civil Engineers (1818), the Law Society (1825), the Royal Institute of British Architects (1852) and the British Medical Association (1856). The simultaneous appearance of the middle-class gentlemen's clubs can be seen as part of the same process, along with the foundation of the Victorian public schools (nine at the beginning of the nineteenth

Bishop of London

Rev. John Rashdall

Rev. Gordon Palmer

Rev. Matthew Burrell.

Some of the numerous clergymen members of the O&C in the nineteenth century: Bishop of London; Rev. John Rashdale; Rev. Gordon Palmer; Rev. Matthew Burrell

century, perhaps two hundred by its end) for the sons of prosperous but unaristocratic fathers. *

'The point of a club', Anthony Sampson observed, writing in
1962, 'is not who it lets in, but who it keeps out.'[4] In the case of
the university clubs the grounds for eligibility have always been
extremely clear and remain so to this day: in most other clubs
they have tended to become hazily indistinct or jocularly ana-
chronistic (as at the Travellers' or the Reform). Even the clubs for
the armed services have in the main thrown their doors wide.
However, eligibility does not confer entitlement: in all three
clubs election was originally by ballot of the members. Twenty
votes were needed and two blackballs excluded. There appears to
be no way of discovering how rigorous a hurdle this was, since
the term 'not elected' in the candidates' books often simply
means 'withdrawn'. In 1892 at the Oxford and Cambridge Club
the committee received two complaints from members that their
candidates for election had been blackballed, both on false
rumours, that one was Jewish and the other was divorced. No
action was taken.[5] A potent reminder of our not-so-distant
imperial past is the question of colour. In 1928 at the same club a
member enquired whether it would be acceptable to put up an
Indian for membership. The committee replied that it would be
permissible under the rules of the club but not advisable.[6] In the
1930s most clubs, the university clubs among them, went over to
election by the committee instead of by ballot of the members,
but still doubts remained about the admission of non-Europeans,
even as guests. At the New University a member wrote in 1933 to
ask whether it would be all right to bring an Indian (a delegate to
the World Economic Conference) to the club. The committee sat
on the fence, saying that, while not encouraging, it would leave
the matter to the member's discretion.[7] As late as 1955 at the
Oxford and Cambridge members of the committee were asked

* A slightly later stage in the process, no doubt greatly assisted by the need of the
political parties for party funds, would be the elevation to what Lady Bracknell called
'the purple of commerce' of the new manufacturing interest – W. H. Smith (Viscount
Hambleden), a stationer and newsagent; Lord Wimborne, steel manufacturer; Lords
Cheylesmore and Rochdale, cotton; Lords Hindlip, Burton and Iveagh, of Allsopp,
Bass and Guinness (known as the Beerage).

'to give some thought to the probable application for membership by gentlemen of non-European extraction'.[8] Three years
later at Suffolk Street a considerable fuss ensued over the non-
election of an African candidate on grounds of colour. Sir Henry
Willink wrote to protest and asked to be allowed to address the
committee on the subject. In the following year a 'committee of
wise men' (distinguished members of the club) was invited to
advise on the admission of such candidates.[9]

'Promoting and continuing a mutual interest and fellowship'
were among the stated objects of the Oxford and Cambridge
Club, but neither this one nor the other two were particularly
social clubs – not at any rate in the sense that the Garrick, say,
or the Savile were and still are: there is no mention, for
example, of a club table in the nineteenth century. Clubs can
be places for getting away from other people as well as for
meeting them. The reason Gladstone preferred Suffolk Street
and would not respond to invitations to joint the Athenaeum
is because he feared that at the latter club members would
bother him, whereas at Suffolk Street he was left in peace. No
doubt friends among fellow-members would meet and chat,
but 'clubbability' in the sense of being sociable was never a
requirement.

What, then, did members seek from their club? Not visitors, at
least in the early days, for as at most clubs the introduction of
strangers was rather discouraged. Not bedrooms, for most
members lived within walking distance or a cab-ride of the club
and for members up from the country nearby lodgings were not
hard to find. Certainly not female company. Somewhere to relax
over the newspapers and periodicals, a good library to read or
doze in, and somewhere to play cards or billiards: most important, somewhere to eat well but cheaply and somewhere with a
decent cellar – these were the main requirements. The things one
would most like to know, though, can never be known – what
members talked about and what influence the clubs may have
exerted on the political and religious issues of the day. As R. H.
Mottram – one of the few historians who considers the question –
has noted,

They [the clubs] present a phenomenon unique in history. For they cannot be dismissed as mere idling places of the rich. They contained many of the best brains in the country as well as some of the nastiest characters. It was with the support of the public they represented that *The Edinburgh Review* went crusading for political reform, *The Quarterly Review* for social reform. The Conservative revival of the thirties was organised from the Carlton; the foundation of the Reform to be a Radical counterweight to the pure Whiggery of Brooks's involved as much agitation as a Cabinet shuffle.[10]

But the historian is constrained by his sources, so the influence of the university clubs can only be a matter for speculation.

Club records are a surer guide to London manners than to ideas. Snuff-taking, once general, was gradually giving way to smoking in Victorian times, despite the Queen's aversion to it. Some clubs, such as the Alfred, banned it entirely – said by some to be the main reason for its demise in 1853. It was White's refusal to allow smoking in the drawing room which led the Prince of Wales to withdraw his candidacy and instead found the Marlborough (referred to by Trollope in several novels as 'The Beargarden', which has 'smoke all over the house'). At the Oxford and Cambridge smoking caused the first major row in the club's history: at an Extraordinary General Meeting in 1831 a motion 'that a Smoking Room be established for the general use and benefit of the Club' was firmly negatived, 98 votes to 50.[11] Five years later, when plans were in hand for the new house at 71 Pall Mall, the committee ordered that a notice be put up in the club rooms: 'The Question as to the propriety of fitting up a Smoking Room in the New Club will be submitted to the consideration of Members at the Annual General Meeting on 25th of May.'[12] At the meeting the motion that there should be a smoking room was narrowly carried (56–52), but the very next day by a requisition of fifty members the matter was referred to a further Special General Meeting. The AGM decision was confirmed (91–76), but when, thirty-one years later, a further requisition signed by fifty-three members asked for consideration to be given to making an extra room available, it was negatived by 107 votes.[13] What is today referred to as the smoking room was originally called the drawing room: only in 1889 was smoking permitted there.[14]

The Great Exhibition is said to have made smoking more widespread – many of the foreign visitors smoked – but did not make it socially acceptable: it was the Prince of Wales who did that and it was the First World War that overcame the last barricades. At the Oxford and Cambridge Club a motion 'that it is desirable that further facilities be afforded for smoking in the Club' in 1917 was passed *nem.con.* By 1935 only the coffee room and the North Library remained sacrosanct. At Suffolk Street up to 1895 smoking was only allowed in the second-floor rooms: by 1917 it was permitted in the drawing room and by 1919 in the Silence Library. At the New University Club the library and the coffee room were by 1920 the only non-smoking rooms: by 1927 only the coffee room held out. Until well past the turn of the century tobacco means for the most part cigars or pipes. The first cigarette factory did not open until 1857 (cigarettes then were twice as thick and half as long again as today, and had a straw or cane mouthpiece): the first reference to any of the clubs stocking them was in 1873 at the NUC.[15] At the Oxford and Cambridge in 1890 the cigar account was given as £78–10s., while the cigarette account stood at only £5–19s.[16]

Dress was a less contentious matter. Up to 1914 top hats and frock coats were the ordinary dress of a gentleman of leisure, especially when the court was in residence. In all clubs except Pratt's members dressed for dinner, though it is alleged that men wore black waistcoats with their tailcoats unless they were going to a dance. The dinner jacket – contemptuously referred to as a bum-freezer – was still rare. Anyone defying the conventions would be taken to task. An entry in the Suffolk Street Suggestion Book dated 1902 proposes 'That members who use the reading room of the Club in bicycle costume should receive an intimation that their knickerbockers and stockings are inappropriate'. At the same club in 1931 a letter from Major Pollock to the committee drew their attention to 'the appearance in the Entrance Hall of the Club at 9.15 p.m. of a young member, who had previously dined, in flannel trousers and a sweater'. The committee replied that they deplored this slackness on the part of this

member, and were in full sympathy with Mr Pollock that such
dress was not in keeping with the traditions of the Club.[17]
Dressing for dinner survived until the Second World War,
though at some stage between the wars it became permissible at
the Oxford and Cambridge Club to 'dine dirty' at one end of the
coffee room. By today's relaxed standards the club's notion of
proper dress is still fairly formal: except at weekends and in the
squash bar a jacket and tie are still *de rigueur* and there is no great
pressure to relax things further – though in 1969 one rebel proposed in the Oxford and Cambridge Club's Suggestion Book

Either: that portraits in the Coffee Room be removed since the
          Members portrayed are not wearing ties
Or: that the Committee reverse so absurd a rule
Or: that Civil Servants shall cease to be Members.

The committee, rather losing their *sang froid*, instructed the
Secretary to delete this entry before replacing the book in the
vestibule.[18]

One sartorial convention which varied from club to club was
the wearing of hats in the club house. In some it was traditional,
in others it was regarded as bad form. The Oriental and the St
James's allowed hats to be worn at breakfast and lunch but not at
dinner. At the NUC in 1865 the committee considered a backed
bill 'recommending that a notice should be put up requesting
gentlemen not to wear hats in the dining room during dinner
time': their reply was that they 'do not think it expedient to put
one up'.[19] Apparently this was not acceptable at the Oxford and
Cambridge Club twenty years later, for on receiving from a
member a complaint that another places his hat on his dinner
table, the committee wrote to him asking him not to.[20] However,
the tradition of wearing hats indoors lingered on at Suffolk Street;
a member reminiscing about the club in the 1940s comments 'My
fellow older members lack the character of our predecessors. I
have yet to see at Pall Mall ancient worthies sitting in "their"
chairs in the morning room or library wearing grey bowler
hats.'[21]

When in 1939 the Suffolk Street Suggestion Book, started in
1881, finally ran out of pages, the last entry was signed by Major

R. H. Sampson. It read:

It is ... suggested that this volume should be carefully preserved. It is a running commentary on the habits and changes of the Club from 1881–1939 and as such, is full of historical interest. It is moreover a mine rich in conscious and unconscious humour, dealing as it does with fads and foibles and periodical petulance as well as constructive assistance and genuine grievance.

Indeed the suggestions, all exercising the clubman's inalienable right to find fault, vary little with the passing of years: the earlier entries tend to be in more spidery writing but are on the whole better spelt. 'I beg to call the attention of the Committee to the quality of the quill pens in the Library' (1884); 'that the Club should be connected with the Telephone System' (1885) leads inevitably to the complaint 'that the growing custom of allowing Ladies to use the Club Telephone should cease' (1928): this attracted seven signatures and the committee so ordered. Talking in the library, the bill of fare and the quality of the coffee are constant themes: so in the earlier years were the subjects of heating, lighting and ventilation (admittedly greater problems in the days of oil and gas lamps, especially when combined with the Victorians' horror of draughts: all the clubs spent large sums on ingenious devices for ventilation, usually fruitlessly, and their remains can be seen at various points in the club house). Members, it seems, have tended to regard umbrellas rather as undergraduates regard bicycles: 'As I have had my umbrella taken from the Club twice *within the last month*, and the Hall Porter informs me that it is the constant practice of members to take away other members' umbrellas, I would suggest that the committee should adopt some means of checking this incipient form of socialism' (1895). But there are limits to what even the most conscientious committee can achieve. *

The reports of the Oxford Union's 'King and Country' debate in 1933 moved one member to suggest 'That the Secretary be requested to complete a list of names including that of the Presi-

---

* Hence the Duke of Wellington's sage advice to the Kildare Club in Dublin: 'Very well, think what you are about; but if you let in the bishops, mind your umbrellas'. (Elizabeth Longford, *Wellington: Pillar of State*, p. 150).

dent of the Oxford Union who has admitted responsibility for the wording of the motion recently carried and confirmed there pledging the members "not to fight for their King and Country under any circumstances", and of the members report in the *Isis* of February 15th as having spoken in favour of the motion; and to bring the matter to the notice of the Committee if the names of any of these gentlemen should appear in the candidates' book.' (The reply was 'The Committee having considered the above suggestion and having heard the opinion of Mr. P. A. Landon of Trinity College, Oxford, are of opinion that the incident at the Oxford Union is not of sufficient importance as to merit their taking any notice of it'.)

In a perfect world all members would behave in a gentlemanly fashion; but as it isn't, they don't. The most frequent form of delinquency in club history is financial. 'Clubs', as Trollope observed, 'are pleasant resorts in all respects but one. They require ready money or even worse than that in respect to annual payments, – money in advance.'[22] The penalty for failure to pay a subscription is and has always been virtually automatic – the member's name is posted on the club notice board and if he remains in default is erased from the list of members. Failure to pay an account (and in London clubs the tradition has always been cash on the nail) is likely to produce a magisterial rebuke from the committee, as happened to Mr Townend at Suffolk Street in 1854:

The Committee of the United University Club regret to learn that Mr Townend has more than once transgressed the Rule prohibiting Members from leaving their dinner bills unpaid. The Committee request Mr Townend to pay the bills now outstanding at once and to forbear from such irregularity in the future.[23]

More pathetic than delinquent, perhaps, is the steady trickle of members whose cheques, usually for minute amounts, bounce when presented to the club's bankers, or – more heinously – are returned by other clubs up and down Pall Mall which have been offering members hospitality during the summer closure. This, unless pre-empted by voluntary resignation, would result in the threat of formal expulsion, as occurred in the case of Mr Dickins in 1854:

The Secretary exhibited a dishonoured cheque for £10 of Mr Dickins' dated 14th Ult. and was directed to write to Mr Dickins, desiring an immediate remittance of the amount to prevent the necessity for ulterior measures which the Committee have in contemplation.[24]

Over-indulgence in alcohol, provided it did not lead to grossly anti-social behaviour, tended to be tolerated, and was in any case much less common than in an earlier age. If, as happened at the Oxford and Cambridge in 1918, a member 'was intoxicated and incapable of behaving like a gentleman', or, as happened to one unfortunate cleric there ten years later, was complained of as being 'hopelessly drunk', they could usually be prevailed on to resign. For obvious reasons, clubs prefer to deal with their internal problems privately and it is only very exceptionally that a full-blown ceremony of expulsion becomes necessary. This did happen however, at the Oxford and Cambridge Club in 1877, when a notice was inserted in *The Times*, the *Daily News* and several other papers to the effect that 'A General Meeting of the Oxford and Cambridge University Club will be held on Wednesday May 2nd 1877 at the Club to consider the conduct of a Member under Rule 52. The Chair will be taken at 4 o'clock p.m.'[25] In fact it all seems to have been a storm in a soup plate, during which one member had lost his temper with another and had called him 'no gentleman', 'a damned snob', and had referred to him to the Steward as 'that blackguard'. The meeting was duly held, with Sir William Harcourt MP in the chair: the conduct of the member in question was held to have been 'injurious to the character and interests of the Club' and the motion that he had merited the penalty of expulsion was passed, 220 votes to 5.

The last occasion on which this cumbrous procedure was used was in 1950 when a member, who was clearly unbalanced, insisted that on numerous occasions his food had been poisoned and his personal effects interfered with. He was duly expelled but the process was so clearly embarrassing that thereafter the rules were changed and such decisions were left to the committee rather than to a general meeting.[26] This brought it into line with the practice at Suffolk Street, where the change had been made in 1923.

Where deviant behaviour can be attributed more to eccentricity than delinquency, particularly in an elderly member, committees have tended to take a lenient view. A member at Suffolk Street reminiscing in the *Club Bulletin* about the 1920s, recalled that

We still had individual hand towels in the lavatories. A club servant going into that department in the course of his work found a member busily stuffing a small suitcase with hand towels and so far forgot himself as to exclaim, 'But Sir, you can't do that!'. The member rounded on him, 'Why not? I always bring them back when they're dirty'.[27]

Committees, Secretaries and Club Servants

In more leisurely times, when the pound retained its value and servants were plentiful, a club, given an efficient secretary, could more or less run itself with just the occasional touch on the tiller from the committee. In the nineteenth century, though committees met weekly from October till July, they were normally not well attended (at Suffolk Street in the 1890s when it met on Thursdays at 5 or 5.30 in the afternoon, it was rare for more than four or six to attend). If some matter of special importance needed discussion a 'special' committee would be called – a device as unknown to club rules as a three-line whip is to the constitution, but with much the same purpose.

That, however, would only be if some specially tendentious item had to be considered, such as 'conduct of a member' or, as happened at Suffolk Street in 1898, when it was found that the club's solicitor had absconded and the office was in the hands of the Official Receiver.[28] Normally the committee had only to concern itself with trivialities. This minute from the New University Club is about typical:

The Secretary reported that Volume 3b of the Justen Society's publication was missing from the Library. The Committee sanctioned the purchase of new shades for the lights in the Strangers' Billiard Room and the construction of a bookcase over the Smoking Cabinets in the corridor. They also decided that plans of the Club should be repaired, framed and glazed, and that notices regarding wet brushes in the lavatory and sticks and umbrellas in the Hall should be put up.[29]

To some extent a committee exists to be sniped at. Major R. H. Sampson ('Richard Hull') was only exaggerating a little when he wrote

There is no more popular target for abuse than the committee of a club. It would be worse than inaccurate, it would be dull, to belong to a club, or for that matter to any other society, and admit that it was at all times perfectly managed. If a body of angels, endowed with perfect wisdom and all the gold wherewith the Streets of Heaven are paved, were to take over the government of the country, they would undoubtedly be defeated at the next election, but if they took over the management of a club, all the members would resign out of pure boredom.[30]

Occasionally a complainant, forgetting perhaps that the committee are not his employees but fellow members like himself, has gone too far and the committee will retaliate, as happened at the Oxford and Cambridge Club in 1832 when they resolved 'That a letter be written to Mr – requesting him to refrain from making his complaints on his Dinner Bills in terms so offensive to the Committee, as he has done'.[31]

On the whole, as has already been observed, members are content to leave the running of a club to the committee, but there have been occasions when its decision in a matter has simply been overruled at a General Meeting. This happened when William Morris, the first Secretary of the Oxford and Cambridge Club, applied in 1844 for an increase in salary from £300 on the grounds that other club secretaries were getting more, that he had been Secretary for the fourteen years since the club's foundation, and that the club's finances could bear it. The committee agreed to an increase of £100. Sixty-one members wrote opposing the increase but the committee stood firm. However, at the next Annual

General Meeting the members voted down the committee's decision and the Secretary's salary reverted to £300.[32] Relations at this time between the committee and the members appear to have been strained, because two years later the committee invited the Earl of Falmouth to become a trustee in the place of the Duke of Buckingham and Chandos, only to have their invitation abruptly negatived at the next AGM.[33] The committee did not resign on that occasion, as one feels they might well have done, but of course they did on another, over a hundred and twenty years later, when the members voted down the committee's proposal to wind up the club.

The device of delegating certain matters to sub-committees consisting of members with particular interests and experience is as old as the clubs themselves: wine, the library, billiards, cigars and the like. Some are in effect standing committees, while others have been appointed on an *ad hoc* basis to deal with particular problems – at the Oxford and Cambridge Club, for example, to consider bedroom accommodation, the installation of electric lighting, the purchase of No. 77 Pall Mall and the admission of ladies.

So far as the general management of the club is concerned, one drawback to the committee is that it is too large. Again to quote Major Sampson on the subject: 'Of course in fact nothing of any real importance occurs at a committee meeting. You cannot expect twenty-four people to meet together and arrive at a sensible decision; the number is far too high. The proceedings, therefore, are in the nature of a formality.'[34] As times became tougher the tendency has been for a smaller, inner committee to evolve, consisting probably of the chairman, the vice-chairman and three or four members with particular legal and financial skills. Though it can by no means take for granted the general committee's acquiescence in all its proposals (any more than the general committee can that of the membership as a whole) this is a system which has worked well and has certainly brought to club management a degree of professionalism and fine tuning on the financial side which would not otherwise have been possible.

One of the most important decisions a committee is ever called

upon to make is the appointment of a secretary, for on him the
efficiency of the club and the happiness of both members and staff
will largely depend. Until very recent times club secretaries have
tended to be retired officers of the armed services. Of the thirty or
so secretaries of the university clubs (it is not possible to be
precise because of certain gaps in the records), some ten have
been retired army or naval officers. In terms of the club records
secretaries tend to be rather shadowy, anonymous figures: unless
they are particularly controversial or thoroughly bad hats, all we
tend to discover is when they were appointed, when they retired
and how much they were paid. Thankfully, there was only one
really bad hat (though he was appointed secretary both at Suffolk
Street and in Pall Mall). A question mark hangs over the latter
club's first secretary, William Morris. Having had his salary so
unceremoniously cut by the AGM in 1845 he nevertheless remained Secretary for another ten years, despite the fact that in
1846 a resolution was passed 'That the Committee desire to
express to the Secretary their continued dissatisfaction with his
general management and superintendence of the affairs of the
Club'.[35] Morris retired in 1855 on a pension of £150 after twenty-
five years as Secretary. However, two years later it transpired
that nearly two thousand bottles of wine were missing from the
club cellars. The butler, who had been stealing it for the past few
years, was sacked, but the committee took the view that the
blame was really Morris's for having condoned the system that
made it possible. A Special General Meeting was called and on
the committee's recommendation a motion 'That the Pension
voted to Mr Morris in the year 1855 be discontinued' was carried
unanimously.[36]

Morris was succeeded by W. H. Thomas, one of 113 candidates who had applied, still at the salary of £300, though this was
raised to £350 when the committee learned that he had applied for
the secretaryship of the Carlton Club. He died in harness after
twenty-five years as secretary in 1881. His successor, W. J.
Woodstock, served even longer: he retired in 1919, aged over
seventy. He appears to have been a paragon among secretaries:
'We may at once anticipate the contents of this report,' the audi-

tors commented in 1910, 'by saying that we think the purchase and handling of Provisions are well and truly looked after. In few Clubs (if indeed in any) of which we have examined the accounts, have we found the records and statistics in better form.' The Secretary was congratulated and awarded an honorarium of fifty guineas. Long service became the hallmark of secretaries at the Oxford and Cambridge Club: with only one exception all subsequent secretaries served the club for over twenty years, whereas the average length of service at the other two clubs was barely ten.

Long and loyal service has always tended to be taken, too, as the hallmark of club servants, and up to a point this is true: the minutes of all three clubs contain many references to the death or retirement of those who had served the club for forty or fifty years, often beginning as page boys and slowly working their way up through the hierarchy, such as W. Dalley, head waiter at the Oxford and Cambridge, a club servant from 1890 to 1938, H. Morgan, carver for forty years, F. Foster, a waiter for fifty, and W. Pullen, coffee room waiter, after fifty-five years' service to the club. At Suffolk Street there was I. Garner, who retired as butler in 1887 after fifty-one years' service, having started as a page boy in 1836, or W. Hart, the club messenger, who was pensioned off at £35 a year (equivalent to his full wages) in 1892 after fifty-five years' service.

However, lest the picture be painted too rosily, it must be said that these were exceptional: many servants seem just to have drifted from club to club as they do today, or into private service or the many hotels and restaurants around the West End. Moreover, there were many cases of dismissal, generally for drunkenness or embezzlement. In 1832 at Suffolk Street the Secretary reported that 'a system of fraud and embezzlement has been found to exist, and is in daily operation by certain of the Footmen employed in the coffee room'.[37] The head waiter and his deputy were sacked. Thirty years later an old servant was prosecuted and many others were sacked for a system of robbery which had probably been going on for some time. In 1901 alone the housekeeper was dismissed for having large deficiencies in her stock of linen and the steward and the chef were dismissed.

Three years later the housekeeper had again to be sacked, this time for drunkenness. At the Oxford and Cambridge Club the drawing room waiter and the under butler were dismissed in the very first months of the club's foundation for 'having improperly conducted themselves'.[38] In 1841 the butler was ordered to leave the house the same night for giving short measure, trying to remove six dozen bottles of wine from the club and being intoxicated.[39] At the NUC there was the sad case of the steward, an old and trusted servant of the club of twenty-five years' standing, who absconded in 1895 with cheques worth £120. His body was found a month later in the Albert Dock in Hull with the cheques still on it.[40] So it went on, though few incidents can have been quite so spectacular as the occasion in Pall Mall in 1969 when one of the cooks had to be removed from the club – an operation which had necessitated an ambulance and nine policemen.[41]

Clubs are and always were considerable employers of labour. In 1914 the Servants' sub-committee at the Oxford and Cambridge Club reported that twelve of the leading clubs in the area employed between them 948 servants. *

The hierarchy and general organisation resembled that in any grand household. For a somewhat earlier period (1843–45) we have a complete breakdown of club servants and their duties at Suffolk Street; at this time, of course, the house was smaller and provided no bedrooms for members. In charge of the direction of the whole establishment under the secretary was the house steward, responsible for the plate, the cellars and the ordering and quality of the food. Next came the butler, responsible under the steward for the dispense cellar and the coffee room. Below him came the under butler, whose duties included the cleaning of the silver and plate and presiding over the servants' hall. He and the lamp man were expected to sleep in the butler's pantry on alternate nights to guard the plate.

* This survey gave the following figures for the three university clubs

Oxford & Cambridge Club	Membership	Servants	Prop. of Members to each Servant
United University Club	1000	62	16.1
Oxford & Cambridge Club	1200	68	17.6
New University Club	1200	59	20.3

Next came the nine footmen or waiters, three attached to the drawing room and libraries and six to the coffee room. The senior drawing room waiter was responsible for returning books to the shelves in the libraries, stitching and distributing the newspapers and arranging the writing materials. The three together would clean the furniture, light up the rooms and carry up the coals. The coffee room waiters, apart from serving the meals, had to carry up the coals for five fires, wash the glass and polish the plate.

The house porter's duties included bringing in all the spring water from Charles Street – three journeys per morning – pumping water from the well, beating the hearth rugs and cleaning the balconies, areas and area steps. The steward's room boy waited on the upper servants who ate in the housekeeper's room rather than in the servants' hall – that is, the steward, the housekeeper, the butler, the cook and the clerk of the kitchen. The lamp man had fifty-seven lamps to clean and prepare as well as replenishing the chandeliers. The hall porter came on duty daily at 6.30 a.m.: he was responsible for regulating the notices, the play bills for the day and the newspapers: he also had charge of all letters, parcels and messages. He was allowed half-an-hour for dinner and half-an-hour for tea, and he went off duty at 9 p.m. He was allowed alternate Sundays off once he had done his morning duty.

In the kitchen department was a cook, a roaster/general assistant (not a qualified cook), two women, the clerk of the kitchen, the sculleryman and the scullerymaid. Under the housekeeper came two still room maids and five housemaids.

The number of servants gradually increased: by 1859 there were forty (twenty-six men and fourteen women): by 1881 there were fifty-two. In accordance with Victorian practice, wages were low and hours were very long. The butler's salary was £70 a year:* a senior coffee room waiter earned £30, a junior one £25. The cook was paid £120 and the clerk of the kitchen £50. A housemaid earned £14 and the humble steward's room boy £6. In addition they all of course received free board and lodging, a quart of mixed ale and porter a day and their livery. With only

---

* For purposes of comparison it should be borne in mind that in 1844 a schoolmaster earned £25 per annum and a schoolmistress £15.

Senior staff of the O&C in 1929

The O&C staff cricket team in 1934

minor adjustments these figures held good till the century had turned.

At the Oxford and Cambridge Club the livery was of blue cloth with white edges and linings and silver buttons, with plush breeches of the same colour. The committee had already decided that servants in livery should wear hair powder, though by the 1830s this was rather going out of fashion: at Suffolk Street it was discontinued in 1833. Livery servants continued to wear breeches until the First World War when the practice was abandoned as an economy measure. Afterwards an attempt at Suffolk Street to revive the practice was unanimously rejected.[42]

There is no reason to think that, despite low pay and long hours, club servants were particularly discontented with their lot: indeed, if they had been they would not have stayed (and even as late as 1934 the average length of service at Suffolk Street was ten years). The job was secure, there were two or three weeks' holiday a year (admittedly on board wages) and the members and committee took a benevolent interest. As early as 1855 the minutes at Suffolk Street record 'That in the opinion of the Committee some steps should be taken to provide a retiring Fund for Old and decayed servants'.[43] Two years later a move was made to set up a staff superannuation fund to which each member of the club would contribute one pound, though it is not clear whether it materialised. In 1892 a Servants' Cricket and General Benevolent Fund – the ancestor of today's Staff Christmas Fund – was established, with a subscription book kept at the desk in the coffee room just as it is today. After the end of the Second World War the Staff Welfare Committee at the Oxford and Cambridge Club reported unfavourably on conditions below stairs: 'The staff conditions in the basement are frankly appalling and it is remarkable that we have ever been able to maintain any staff with such deplorable surroundings. The hostel and bedroom accommodation are not as good as they should be: they lack any comfort.'[44] This was, however, at the end of six years of war; and the committee recommended complete redecoration and new furniture straight away.

Strangers and Ladies

In no respect have clubs changed more than in their attitude to visitors. Today a club's main function is as a place to entertain, but this was not originally the case. The Guards' Club allowed no strangers at all till 1901: the Carlton allowed them no further than the hall: the Athenaeum allowed them in one small room near the entrance. At Suffolk Street members were by 1836 permitted to introduce Oxford and Cambridge members as guests, but not to use the coffee room during the Parliamentary session.* At the Annual General Meeting in 1838 a proposal that up to twenty strangers should be admitted to the coffee room as guests was negatived. It was not until 1853 that a motion was passed to open one room to strangers to dine: even then, no member was to introduce more than two. It inevitably followed that, having asked a guest to dine, you must have somewhere to take him before and after dinner. In 1855 it was grudgingly conceded that you could take him to the drawing room before dinner and to the smoking room afterwards, but to no other rooms. In 1862 it was proposed that strangers be admitted to breakfast as well as dinner but the proposal was lost: it was not till 1891 that it was permissible to entertain strangers to breakfast between 9 a.m. and 1 p.m.

Things were just as restrictive in Pall Mall: at the Annual General meeting in 1848 it was proposed 'That each Member be permitted to introduce one stranger into the House Dining Room subject to such regulations in regard to the numbers to be introduced on each day as to the charge for the table, as the Committee shall think proper': it was negatived, 67 votes to 43.[45] Only reluctantly in the following year was anything further done: the committee conceded that up to six members were to be allowed to introduce up to two strangers on the same day. Their names, addresses and the name of the member had to be entered in a book by 5 p.m.: strangers were to be admitted to the house dining room only (what is now the wine bar) and to the back

---

* To a marked degree club life revolved around the Parliamentary session, which ran, with short breaks for Easter and Whitsuntide, from February to July (Autumn sessions were rare). During it, clubs opened earlier in the day and closed later. This made good sense in the early days when many members were MPs.

writing room beforehand. No one, the committee thoughtfully
added, who had been blackballed was to be invited. The restrictions about where strangers could be taken were gradually relaxed, but it was not till 1876 that it became permissible to entertain strangers to breakfast or lunch, and the same limit on
numbers still applied. Not until 1935 could strangers be given
dinner in the coffee room. Only in 1947, when the strangers'
dining room was required for another purpose, did the concept
of a separate dining room for strangers finally disappear.

Only one account has come to light of what it was like to be
entertained at the United University Club:

I took pleasure in the society of Mr Ellerton, a dignified, agreeable
man, the brother-in-law of Lord Brougham ... He was also the only
Englishman who honoured me by any hospitality, and by
entertaining myself and my friends at the University Club, gave me
an opportunity of realising the munificence of such an establishment
in London. After we had spent a very agreeable time there, I had a
glimpse of the weaker side of English hospitalities of this order,
though the incident was friendly enough. My host had to be taken
home by two men, one holding each arm, quite as a matter of course,
as it was obvious that he could not have got far across the road
without help.[46]

Mr Ellerton's guest on this occasion was Richard Wagner.

'A club,' according to George Augustus Sala, 'is a weapon used
by savages to keep the white woman at a distance.'[47] At least one
contributor to the Suggestion Book at Suffolk Street agreed:
'That no female strangers be admitted to the Club. The admission
of ladies is entirely contrary to the constitution, the traditions
and the rules and regulations of the Club'. The suggestion is
dated 1903; but in fact the member making it was wrong, for the
United University Club was one of the very first to admit ladies.
To begin with it was only for special occasions, such as coronations and funeral processions and royal weddings, but by the
turn of the century they could be admitted to the coffee room for
tea. In 1926 a poll was held on the question of entertaining ladies
in the club: 560 voted in favour, only 124 against. In 1940, when
the new ladies' wing was completed, two hundred lady associates

were elected from among the wives, daughters, sisters and mothers of members. Things were not so different at the Oxford and Cambridge Club: by 1899 ladies calling on members could not venture further than the vestibule, but a proposal 'that ladies, when accompanied by a member, may be shown over the Club, between the hours of 10 a.m. and 1 p.m.' was passed *nem. con.*[48] At some date between the wars – probably in the early 1930s – space was found for a ladies' annex and cocktail bar just to the right of the vestibule on the ground floor, but it was not until 1951 when the club acquired No. 77 Pall Mall that adequate accommodation was available and lady associates could be elected. At the New University Club it did not happen at all because there simply was not room enough, though the committee tried more than once to find an adjacent or nearby house for the purpose. It is probably true to say that in all cases committees were motivated more by the prospect of economic advantage than by egalitarian principle.

Eating and Drinking

Since clubs are essentially about eating and drinking, it is perhaps surprising that even as late as 1864 when the New University Club was founded, its rules and regulations make no reference to luncheon. This meal made its appearance only slowly as the century proceeded and as the customary hour for dinner got later, and to begin with it tended to be an austere meal, little more than a snack to bridge the gap between breakfast and dinner. In 1833 the committee in Pall Mall resolved 'That either a bason of soup, a sandwich or a Mutton Chop may be had at any hour as luncheon'.[49] The coffee room accounts at Suffolk Street for 1842 show that only about half as many members took luncheon as dined and that the average cost of luncheon was only 8d (as opposed to 2/11 for dinner and 1/6 for breakfast).

Coffee rooms remained open all day and far into the night: in 1885 the committee at Suffolk Street decided that the kitchen would close in future at 1 a.m. throughout the year. Only as a war economy in 1915 was the hour of closing brought forward to

10 p.m. Breakfast could be taken at any time between the hour the club opened (8 a.m., or 9 a.m. from Michaelmas to Lady Day) and 12 noon. Thereafter, luncheon prices (*à la carte*) were charged until 4 p.m. Any meal ordered after four o'clock was charged at dinner prices (which included 6d table money). In 1831 joints were provided in the coffee room at the Oxford and Cambridge Club at 5.15, 5.45, 6.15 and 7.30. By 1883 the hour had become later: a club dinner consisting of soup, fish, entrée, joint and a sweet was served between 6.30 and 8.30 at the price of 3/6, though of course members could dine *à la carte* both earlier and later. At Suffolk Street by 1913 the hours for dinner were still 4 p.m. till 9 p.m., with a club dinner being served between 7 and 8.30: thereafter, supper was served from 9 p.m. till midnight. As the years passed, the number of luncheons served overtook the number of dinners: in Pall Mall in 1897 13,501 members dined and 17,874 took luncheon. By 1905 the figures were 13,012 and 23,097 respectively.

Meals were cheap because there was no attempt to make a profit. A sub-committee on Expenditure reported in 1908 that the average charge for lunches was 1/3: the actual cost to the club was 11½d to 1/3½d. 'We have compared our tariff with those of many other clubs, and can say, without hesitation, that our price for cold table and mutton chops are so low as to make it impossible for any profit to be left, or indeed, to make a loss.'[50]

Tastes have probably not changed all that much over the decades, though menus tend to be longer now to allow for the increased use of clubs for entertaining guests: however, there are some dishes in earlier times which would not appear today. According to T. H. S. Escott, 'Lampreys, Jersey Mullet and lark pudding were dainties brought into favour at the older club by Lord Melbourne's taste and a special gift for preparing them possessed by its cook. Menus of the thirties and forties in which they appear were preserved by old members living into comparatively recent times.'[51] There is mention, too, in the 1870s and 1880s of eel pie, ptarmigan pie, larks and golden plover. *

---

* A request from a member at the Oxford and Cambridge Club in 1907 'that song birds do not appear on the daily bill of fare' was rejected by the committee: 'many members like larks'.

A practice long forgotten but which seems to have been followed by all three clubs was that of members sending their own cooks to work for a while in the club kitchens as 'improvers': they could thereby learn how to cook their employers' favourite dishes. An entry in the Suffolk Street minutes for 1854 draws attention to the cost:

It having been represented to the Committee that Mr Tyrell's cook has been in the kitchen for improvement during nearly eight weeks
Resolved
That the Steward be instructed to inform members who desire to send their cooks to the club to perfect themselves in the art that they cannot be allowed to remain longer than six weeks.[52]

The system seems to have been that the member paid a guinea a week to the chef: lodging was provided by the club with married members of staff. The arrangement appears to have been a popular one with both sides: in 1859 a member seeking a similar arrangement had to be refused by the committee because there were no vacancies. In 1868 the cook at the New University Club asked for and was granted permission to take up to two improvers. It is not clear when this mutually beneficial practice died out. Nowadays, most members would presumably have to send their wives.

All clubs have their ups and downs and the quality of club cooking is not invariably good. In 1834 the committee at Suffolk Street had occasion to reprove the cook:

In consequence of the complaints of this week, and on former occasions, of the great neglect of the cooks in sending up the plain joints very badly dressed;
Resolved
That the Cook be severely reprimanded, and He being called before the Committee, was accordingly severely reprimanded by the Chairman.[53]

The traditional manner of complaining about the cooking was to back one's bill: sometimes there were compliments, but usually a steady drizzle of discontent. Thus, from the Oxford and Cambridge Club in the 1960s:

Onion in the turtle soup

Cauliflower uneatable; no sherry in trifle

Bone splinters in the Shepherd's Pie

No Oriental Salt

Trout tasteless

No Samba tray available

Solder in the savoury (this last from the Bishop of Dorchester).

Whatever the shortcomings of the kitchen, no one could complain about the cellar. Beer or porter was provided free to members both at Suffolk Street and Pall Mall with luncheon or dinner (if called for alone it was 2d a glass): in 1902 a letter addressed to the committee at the latter club suggested that in view of the financial depression in the club's affairs the practice of supplying it *gratis* should be discontinued: the committee disagreed, saying it would only save about fifty pounds a year and had been the custom since the club was founded. However, in the following year it was mooted that ale, porter and barley water should be charged for (1d. a glass for ale or porter, 1d. a carafe for barley water): it is not clear whether this was acted on or not. At Suffolk Street the custom of free beer seems to have continued until at least 1920.[54]

All writers about clubs speak with respect about the wines stocked by both: Escott comments on the bottles of 'priceless' sherry at the Oxford and Cambridge Club, the same as that produced by the City of London at the banquet to the Queen and Prince Albert in 1840: Lord Ducie ('by far the best judge of Claret then living') laid the foundations of the Suffolk Street cellar. Both clubs, he adds, bought with such success because the connoisseurs personally superintended the business: they drained the market of the 1811 hock and the 1834 claret ('to the infinite chagrin of the Travellers' and White's').[55] A surviving wine list from Pall Mall dated about 1870 appears to confirm this excellence. There were a dozen vintage ports, the oldest being Christopher's 1820 (21/- a bottle) and the cheapest Christopher's 1858 (4/-). The clarets included Ch. Léoville

1862 (6/-) and a Ch. Lafite of the same year (7/-). Burgundies included a Montrachet 1858. There were no less than twenty-three champagnes. By 1906 this had grown to twenty-six, with the same number of vintage ports.[56] At Suffolk Street in the 1880s, it is recorded, champagne accounted for 45% of all wine consumed).

Modern wine committees, though, constrained by rocketing prices of clarets, burgundies and champagnes to search further afield even unto the Antipodes, are not all that far ahead of the New University Club, where it was reported in 1898 that 'the wine sent from Australia by Mr. C. C. Webster had arrived'.[57]

All Mod. Cons

The Regency and early Victorian world in which the university clubs were founded may have been in some respects the age of elegance, but in terms of domestic convenience London was still closer to medieval times than to the twentieth century. The clubs' water was drawn from wells or from nearby springs; even the grandest houses were reliant on their cess pools (Wilkins's original club house was not connected to the sewage system until 1849); London was entirely dependent on horse-drawn transport, and there were constant complaints at the UUC about the effluvium from the stables at the rear: in Pall Mall the Oxford and Cambridge Club had to employ a crossing sweeper at 2/- a week to clear away the miasma of mud and horse-droppings so that members could cross the street.

Though Pall Mall (or rather a short section of it) was in 1807 the first street in London to be lit by gas, the Suffolk Street club house appears to have been wholly lit by lamps and candles until the 1830s, for lack of a public supply. When Smirke built the Oxford and Cambridge Club, gas lighting was installed only in the basement and mezzanine. Otherwise, it was candles and lamps – sperm oil in winter and olive oil in the summer months. In 1846 the committee decided to light more of the club by gas, but not the principal rooms. At a meeting

The club staff in 1982
Back row (left to right): D. J. McDougall 1970; R. P. Liddle 1973; J. W.
Mitchell 1974; R. J. Morrison 1978; J. M. Chandler 1974; D. C. Rice 1980;
J. P. Cooney 1973; V. J. Luck 1972; T. A. Hubbard 1978; D. F. Gwynne 1979.
Seated (left to right): M. M. Fish 1976; C. A. Heaney 1981; M. A. Woods
1978; C. P. Clarke 1970; D. B. Valentine 1977; M. R. Torr 1980;
J. McDonald 1982.

The club staff in 1991
Back row (left to right): D. J. M. McDougall 1970; M. Eleveld 1990; W.
Kozyra 1990; W. F. Parkinson 1988; A. E. Magee 1981; J. P. Cooney 1973;
A. W. Beven 1988; D. B. Valentine 1977; D. F. Gwynne 1979.
Seated (left to right): J. L. Duffy 1990; S. Seddon 1990; M. V. Loftus 1990;
M. L. Oro-Cabanas 1978; S. L. Bragg 1985.

in 1855 they resolved 'That the House Committee be requested to take into consideration the Lighting of the Morning and Coffee Rooms and to report upon the possible cost of setting up Gas Lights instead of Oil Lamps'.[58] Eventually in 1860 the coffee room was so lit, though not to everyone's satisfaction, for there were ventilation problems. A motion was proposed at the AGM in 1861

That in consequence of the great inconvenience experienced by Members of this Club from Gas, and the failure of improved means of Ventilation introduced last year, Wax lights be introduced into the Coffee Room.

It was voted down, but only by a small majority of 43 against 37. Four years earlier gas lighting had been extended to the drawing room, though this had been opposed by the club architect, Sydney Smirke: in 1858 it was decided to light the library by gas, by adapting the existing chandelier.

At the end of 1886 a sub-committee was appointed 'to consider the practicability and expense of lighting the Club with the Electric Light': they rejected the idea at first because of the lack of experience of its practicability and the fact that there was so far no external supply: a gas or steam generator would have been needed.* By 1889 they had changed their minds and installed electric light in the morning and coffee rooms. Ten years later it was extended to the hall, the staircase, the mezzanine and the basement. Suffolk Street had decided to do so in 1892.

In 1888 the committee at the Oxford and Cambridge Club received a letter from a member suggesting the club 'should be attached to the Telephonic system' but they unanimously turned the idea down flat. Three years later they received a further request: again they refused. Only in 1898 did they rather reluctantly give way, but stipulated that it should be kept in a 'silent cabinet' (Suffolk Street followed suit in 1900). One unforeseen result quickly appeared: 'In consequence of the decrease in emoluments of the Commissionaire owing to cheap telegrams, tele-

---

* It had already been adopted, though, at the Athenaeum, the Naval and Military and the Junior Carlton Clubs.

phones, etc. and the difficulty in getting a man, the rate of wages was increased by 2/6 a week.'

With the installation in 1900 of a hydraulic-powered lift the twentieth century had really arrived. But who could have guessed that in fifty years' time there would be a television set in the cocktail bar and in seventy-five years' time a computer in the membership secretary's office?

Notes to Chapter VI

1. Quoted by R. H. Mottram, 'Town Life and London' in G. M. Young (ed.).
   Early Victorian England, 1830–65, vol.
   They were namely – Albion, Alfred's, Athenaeum, Boodle's, Brooks's, Carlton,
   Clarence, Cocoa Tree, Dilettanti, Garrick, Graham's, Guards', Oriental, Oxford
   and Cambridge, Portland, Royal Naval, Travellers', Union, United Service,
   Junior United Service, [United] University, West India, White's, Wyndham's
2. T. H. S. Escott. *Club Makers and Club Members*, p. 238
3. Anthony Trollope. *The Way We Live Now*, OUP (world's Classics ed. 1982),
   vol. 1, p. 116
4. Anthony Sampson, *The Anatomy of Britain*, p. 67
5. OC GCM, 11 March 1892
6. OC GCM, 4 July 1928
7. NUC GCM, 19 June 1933
8. OC GCM, 7 December 1955
9. UUC GCM, 26 March and 8 October 1958, 28 January 1959
10. Mottram. *op. cit.*, pp. 182–3
11. OC EGMM, 24 June 1831
12. OC GCM, 17 May 1836
13. OC GCM, 21 June 1867
14. OC AGMM, 17 May 1889
15. NUC GCM, 4 February 1873
16. OC GCM, 10 January 1890
17. UUC GCM, 10 June 1931
18. OC GCM, 29 July 1969
19. NUC GCM, 23 May 1865
20. OC GCM, 14 May 1886
21. Dr Malcolm Graeme. 'Suffolk Street in the 1940's, *Club News* No. 57 July 1988
22. Trollope. *op. cit.*, vol. 1, p. 23
23. UUC GCM, 13 april 1854
24. UUC GCM, 13 August 1854
25. OC GCM, 13 April 1877; SGM, 2 May 1877
26. OC EGMM, 16 February 1950
27. Mr J. S. Gordon Clark. *Club Bulletin* No. 13 July 1975
28. UUC GCM, 30 March 1898
29. NUC GCM, 20 November 1900
30. Richard Hull. *Keep It Quiet*, Penguin ed., p. 66
31. OC GCM, 30 August 1832
32. OC GCM, 10 July 1844; AGM 31 May 1845
33. OC GCM, 27 January 1847: AGM 31 May 1847
34. Hull. *op. cit.*, p. 67
35. OC GCM, 11 November 1846
36. OC SGMM, 21 December 1857
37. UUC GCM, 18 April 1832
38. OC GCM, 24 July 1830
39. OC GCM, 12 March 1841
40. NUC GCM, 12 November and 10 December 1895
41. OC Finance and Genenral Purposes Committee Minutes, 29 September 1969
42. UUC GCM, 23 October 1929
43. UUC GCM, 16 March 1855

44. OC GCM, 5 June 1946
45. OC AGMM, 29 May 1848
46. 1911 ed. of Richard Wagner's autobiography, quoted in *Club Bulletin* No. 11 January 1975
47. Quoted in Ralph Nevill. *London Clubs; Their History and Treasures*, p. 135
48. OC GCM, 1 December 1899
49. IC GCM, 25 April 1833
50. OC Report of Sub-Committee on Expenditure, 19 September 1908
51. Escott. *op. cit.*, pp. 245–6
52. UUC GCM, 25 May 1854
53. UUC GCM, 5 February 1834
54. UUC AGMM, 20 May 1920
55. Escott. *op. cit.* , pp. 245–6
56. *Club Bulletin* No. 18 November 1976
57. NUC GCM, 26 July 1898
58. OC GCM, 2 November 1855

Appendix

A Note on Some of the Contents of the Club House by the late John Nevinson

In the course of the club's life of more than 150 years it is natural that a number of possessions of special interest should have been collected. The library has long been the club's particular pride, and today it comprises some 25,000 volumes, having been enriched by the addition of thousands of books from Suffolk Street. Since the end of the restoration work in 1974 the whole of the contents of the library has been re-catalogued. Apart from the smoking room, the library occupies the entire first floor, including the beautiful South Library, which looks out on Marlborough House, the North Library, which faces Pall Mall and the small Silence Library at the back of the building. Books are also placed in special glass-fronted cases in the smoking room, and on open shelves in the landing leading to the Silence Library and the librarian's room.

The library's great strength is in its collection of books on the life and history of the two senior universities and the public schools. The life and politics of the nineteenth and twentieth centuries and classical and modern literature are well represented, and there is also a fine collection of works on London.

The club has an interesting series of portraits of former members, the most conspicuous being that of the Duke of Wellington, by John Lucas, specially commissioned in 1841. Most of them were 'presented by a member' whose anonymity in each case is respected in the following list.

King Edward VII	½ length in Robes of the Order of the Garter by Sir Arthur Cope.
Clement Attlee	(1883–1964) seated at desk by R. Moynihan 1947.
George Canning	(1709–1827). ¾ length standing by table. Copy after Sir Thomas Lawrence. Original in National Portrait Gallery. 1832.
William Cavendish	7th Duke of Devonshire (1808–1891). ½ length seated, as Chancellor of the University of Cambridge. c. 1885.
W. E. Gladstone	(1809–1898). ¾ length standing. Version of portrait by Sir John Millais.
Charles Grey	2nd Earl Grey (1794–1945). ½ length. Copy after Sir Thomas Lawrence. Original in National Portrait Gallery.
Sir Edward Grey	1st Viscount Grey of Fallodon (1862–1933) by Harold Speed (signed).
Sir William Vernon Harcourt	(1827–1904). ¾ length after original by A. S. Cope 1907 in the National Liberal Club.
Sir John Mowbray	(1815–1899) 'Father of the House of Commons'. Style of G. F. Watts.
John Scott	1st Earl of Eldon (1751–1838). ½ length seated, by or after Sir Thomas Lawrence.
Archibald Tait	(1811–1882). Archbishop of Canterbury. ½ length reproduction of portrait by G. Richmond.
Rev. Montague James Taylor	½ length signed by W. W. Ouless, RA, 1885.
Henry John Temple	3rd Viscount Palmerston (1784–1865). ¾ length by George Smith.
Arthur Wellesley	Duke of Wellington (1769–1852). Full length in robes of Chancellor of the University of Oxford by John Lucas, 1841.

HRH Prince Philip   Duke of Edinburgh by Aubrey
                           Davidson-Houston.

Harold Macmillan   1st Earl of Stockton by Charles Mackinnon,
                           after James Gunn.

Roy Jenkins   Baron Jenkins of Hillhead by David Poole.

The club has a remarkable collection of watercolours of Oxford and Cambridge, many of which are exceptionally fine. A series of five large views of Oxford by Thomas Walton is notable. Views of Cambridge, many attributed to R. B. Harrada, include a distant view of Cambridge and of Caius and King's Colleges from the Backs. William Turner of Oxford is represented by a view of Magdalen Bridge from the East. G. Pine in 1847 painted Christ Church Cloisters and in 1848 Christ Church, Peckwater Quad. There is also a painting by Pugin of the Hall of University College which was done for Ackermann's *Oxford*. Walcott has a view of King's College, Cambridge.

The club also has an almost complete set of the *Oxford Almanacks* from 1719 to the present day. Brought from the United University Club, about 100 of these are framed and hung in various parts of the club. The collection is believed to be the most complete and valuable set in existence.

The club and its predecessors were lavishly provided with table silver and silver plate. Very little of this is still in use, with the exception of some of the small candlesticks which stand on tables in the coffee room. These were acquired in Victorian times when Georgian silver was to be had very cheaply, and as a result the club still has upwards of three dozen, mostly hall-marked and dated in the last years of George II and early George III. The best of these, in sets of four by John Cafe, hallmarked 1759–1760, are kept available for use on special occasions.

One more work of art needs special mention. At the half-landing of the main staircase stands a fine bronze cast of Donatello's David, the original of which, dating from about 1430, was made for Cosimo de' Medici and is now in the Bargello (Museo Nazionale) at Florence. The copy formerly stood in a special niche at the foot of Blomfield's staircase in the United University Club.

Bibliography

A. Unpublished Sources

(All unpublished sources cited here are now held in the archives of the United Oxford and Cambridge University Club).

United University Club

Candidates' Books, 1822–1971
Letter Books Nos 1–39
General Committee Minutes, 1830–1972 (volumes for 1821–29 (volumes for 1821–29, 1833–41 and 1853 missing) 15 volumes
Rules, by-laws, lists of members, etc. 1822, 1931–70
Yearly Minute Books of General Meetings, 1824–1939. 3 volumes
Suggestion Book 1881–1939
Portraits of Members who lost Their Lives in the War 1914–19
Club Bulletin Nos 1–7, July 1970–January 1972

Oxford and Cambridge University Club

Candidates' Books, 1830–1935
General Committee Minutes (including Annual, Extraordinary and Special General Meetings, Chairmen's Reports and Accounts) 1830–1972 (volume for 1931–33 missing) 32 volumes

Finance and General Purposes Committee Minutes, 1961–72, 2
  volumes
Portraits of Members. 2 volumes
Rules, Regulations, list of members, etc. 1839, 1927–1972
The Members of the Oxford and Cambridge University Club
  from its foundation in 1830 to 1924. Volume 2, K-Z (volume 1
  missing)

New University Club

Candidates' Books, 1868–1938
Nominated Candidates, 1914–32. 2 volumes
List of Members, 1864–1937
General Committee Minutes, 1864–1938 (volumes for 1876–92
  and 1903–18 missing). 4 volumes

United Oxford and Cambridge University Club

General Committee Minutes since 1971
Management Committee Minutes since 1974
Club Bulletin/Club News Nos 1–58 April 1972–November 1988

Published Sources

BARKER, Felix and JACKSON, Peter. *The History of London in
  Maps*. Barrie & Jenkins 1990.
BOULTON, William B. *The Amusements of Old London*, 2 vols,
  John Nimmo MDCCCCI
BRITTON, J. and PUGIN, A. *Public Buildings of London*, vol. II.
  John Weale, 2nd enlarged ed. 1838
BUCHAN, J. *Memory Hold-The-Door*. Hodder & Stoughton
  1940
BURFORD, E. J. *Royal St James's*. Robert Hale 1988
BUTLER, David and SLOMAN, Anne. *British Political Facts
  1900–1979*. Macmillan, 5th ed. 1980
CHANCELLOR, E. Beresford. *Memorials of St James's Street*.
  Grant Richards Ltd 1922

CRAWLEY, Charles. *Trinity Hall.* CUP for Trinity Hall 1976

Dictionary of National Biography and Supplements

ENSOR, R. C. K. *England 1870–1914.* OUP 1936

ESCOTT, T. H. S. *Club Makers and Club Members.* Fisher Unwin 1914

FORREST, Denys. *Foursome in St James's: The Story of the East India, Devonshire, Sports and Public Schools Club.* Privately printed 1982

GATER, Sir George and GODFREY, Walter H. (ed.). *Survey of London: vol. xx Parish of St Martin-in-the-Fields, Pt. III: Trafalgar Square and Neighbourhood.* LCC 1940

GATHORNE-HARDY, Jonathan. *The Public School Phenomenon 1597–1955.* Hodder & Stoughton 1977

GRAVES, Charles. *Leather Armchairs.* Cassell 1963

GRIFFITHS, A. G. F. *Clubs and Clubmen.* Hutchinson 1907

HULL, Richard [Major R. H. Sampson]. *Keep It Quiet.* Faber 1935

KELLAS, Arthur. *Down to Earth.* Pentland Press (Edinburgh) 1990

LACEY, Robert. *Aristocrats.* Hutchinson/BBC 1985

LEJEUNE, Anthony. *The Gentlemen's Clubs of London.* Macdonald & Jane's 1979

LONGFORD, Elizabeth. *Wellington: Pillar of State.* Weidenfeld & Nicholson 1972

McCARTHY, Justin. *A Short History of Our Own Times.* Chatto & Windus, rev.ed. 1923

MACMICHAEL, J. Holden. *The Story of Charing Cross and its Immediate Neighbourhood.* Chatto & Windus 1906

MAGNUS, Philip. *Gladstone.* Murray 1954

MARIE LOUISE, Princess. *My Memories of Six Reigns.* Evans Brothers 1956

MASON, Philip. *The English Gentleman.* André Deutsch 1982

MORLEY, John. *The Life of William Ewart Gladstone, Vol. 1.* Macmillan 1903

MURPHY, N. T. P. *One Man's London.* Hutchinson 1989

NEVILL, Ralph. *London Clubs, their History and Treasures.* Chatto & Windus 1911

PETRIE, Sir Charles. *The Carlton Club*. Eyre & Spottiswoode 1955

PETRIE, Sir Charles. *Scenes of Edwardian Life*. Eyre & Spottiswoode 1965

PETRIE, Sir Charles. *The Victorians*. Eyre & Spottiswoode 1960

PEVSNER, Nikolaus. *The Buildings of England. vol. 1. The Cities of London and Westminster*. Penguin 1957

PIPER, David. *Companion Guide to London*. Collins 1964

POPE-HENNESSY, James. *Monckton Milnes*, 2 vols. Constable 1949 and 1951

RICHARDS, J. M. (ed.). *Who's Who in Architecture*. Weidenfeld & Nicholson 1977

SAMPSON, Anthony. *The Anatomy of Britain*. Hodder & Stoughton 1962

SCOTT, J. M. *The Book of Pall Mall*. Heinemann 1965

SHANNON, Richard. *Gladstone, vol. 1*. Hamish Hamilton 1982

SHEPPARD, F. H. W. (ed.). *Survey of London: vol. xxix The Parish of St. James Westminster. Pt 1: South of Piccadilly*. Athlone Press for LCC 1960

SHUTE, Nevil [Lt-Cdr N. S. Norway]. *Pied Piper*. Heinemann 1942

SHUTE, Nevil. *Slide Rule*. Heinemann 1954

SHUTE, Nevil. *A Town Like Alice*. Heinemann 1950

SIMS, George R. (ed.). *Edwardian London, vol. 1*. Cassell 1902

SUMMERSON, John. *Architecture in Britain 1530–1830*. Penguin 1953

TERRAINE, John. *The First World War 1914–18*. Hutchinson 1965; Macmillan p.b. 1984

TIMBS, John. *Clubs and Club Life in London*. Chatto & Windus 1872

TSUZUKI, Chuschicki. *H. M. Hyndman and British Socialism*. OUP 1961

WHEATLEY, Henry B. *London Past and Present*, 3 vols. John Murray 1891

WHEATLEY, Henry B. *Round About Piccadilly and Pall Mall or, A Ramble from the Haymarket to Hyde Park*. Smith, Elder & Co. 1870

WOLFENDEN, Lord. *Turning Points*. The Bodley Head 1976

WOODBRIDGE, George. *The Reform Club 1836–1978*. Members of the Reform Club in association with Clearwater Publishing Inc. 1978

WOODWARD, E. L. *The Age of Reform 1815–70*. OUP 1938

WRIGHT, Peter. *Spycatcher*. Viking/Penguin, New York 1987

YOUNG, G. M. (ed.). *Early Victorian England 1830–65*, 2 vols. OUP 1934

Index

Note: Page numbers *in italics* refer to illustrations. n after a page number indicates a footnote. WWI and WWII stand for World War I and World War II. NUC stands for New University Club: O&C for Oxford and Cambridge University club: UUC for United University Club.